THE POWER OF KABBALAH

SECRETS OF THE UNIVERSE

& PRINCIPLES OF LIFE

POWER OF
KABBALAH

RABBI YEHUDA BERG

For further information:

The Kabbalah Centre™
Director Rav Berg

1-800-KABBALAH™
www.kabbalah.com™
14 Ben Ami St., Tel Aviv, Israel 63342
155 E. 48th, New York City, NY 10017
1062 S. Robertson Blvd., Los Angeles, CA 90035

—————•◆•—————

First Edition
September 2000
Printed in Canada

ISBN 1-57189-180-3

TO *M*ICHAL-
MY WIFE AND THE MOTHER
OF MY CHILDREN,
YOU ARE THE LIGHT OF MY LIFE,
THE CENTER OF MY UNIVERSE
AND MY HEART OF HEARTS.
TO MY PARENTS-
WHOSE UNCONDITIONAL LOVE
AND SPIRITUAL GUIDANCE
HAVE BEEN MY INSPIRATION.
AND TO MICHAEL-
YOU ARE NOT ONLY THE BEST
BROTHER ANYONE COULD HAVE,
BUT ALSO MY BEST FRIEND.

Dedicated
for the elevation of the soul of
לע'ילוּי נשׁמת
מרדכי בן רוזמים קפשׁ

Blessing for health, success
and happiness for
Beman Bat Yochanan
Zarintaj Bat Mordechai
Nejat Ben Yaakov.

CONTENTS

A student approaches his revered teacher and asks him to reveal all the sublime secrets and magnificent mysteries of the cosmos in the short time that it takes to remain balanced on one leg. This eminent master is one of the greatest spiritual giants to ever walk this earth. Upon hearing his eager student's request, he considers the question very carefully. His eyes then sparkle with infinite wisdom.

A FOUNTAINHEAD OF WISDOM

Suppose there was a hidden wisdom that revealed and unified the spiritual and physical laws of life...

Suppose this wisdom was the true source of all spiritual teachings on this planet, predating religion, Adam and Eve, and even Creation of the world itself...

Suppose its insights had a profound influence on the foremost thinkers throughout history...

Suppose a small circle of eminent sages had long ago grasped this wisdom and recorded it in books that were concealed for two millennia...

Finally, suppose this hidden wisdom revealed all the secrets of the universe, all the answers to your questions, all the solutions to your problems...

This wisdom exists, though it's been kept under wraps throughout much of human history. The wisdom is called Kabbalah, and the visionaries who dared to contemplate and expound upon its mysteries were known as Kabbalists.

The major text of Kabbalah is called the *Zohar*,

and its mystical teachings have influenced the world's most brilliant spiritual, philosophical, religious, and scientific minds— something unknown to humanity at large.

THE SECRET'S OUT

The process of bringing this wisdom into the hands of people just like you began some 2,000 years ago, with the books of the *Zohar*, the authoritative body of knowledge on Kabbalah, and their author, a giant among Kabbalists, Rabbi Shimon bar Yochai. During the centuries that followed, a long line of courageous Kabbalists were scorned by the religious establishment for their efforts to make Kabbalah and the teachings of the *Zohar* available and accessible to people from all walks of life. Blood was spilled, and lives were tragically ruined. Ironically, after their passing, these same Kabbalists were suddenly held in the highest esteem by those who had spurned them. This has been the pattern for over 20 centuries. You are now able to read this book of a long-lost wisdom thanks, primarily, to three men. They are the true Kabbalists of our era:

Kabbalist Rav Ashlag

Kabbalist Rav Brandwein

Kabbalist Rav Berg

I'm proud to say that Rav Berg is also my father, my teacher, my mentor and my friend. Rav Brandwein was my father's master and Rav Ashlag was Rav Brandwein's beloved teacher.

The true distinction of these men is their uncommon ability to make esoteric and complex teachings intelligible to the layperson. Throughout history, scientists, philosophers, and physicians secretly probed Kabbalah for ideas and notions that eventually helped shape the leading philosophical and scientific doctrines. Scholars explored Kabbalah for intellectual and academic purposes. But while one may be a brilliant scholar of classical music, only a Mozart can compose a symphonic masterpiece. Rav Berg, Rav Brandwein, and Rav Ashlag are the true modern day virtuosos of Kabbalah, the authentic custodians of this wisdom. Their lineage dates back to the time of Abraham, through a time-honored lineage that preserved the wisdom in its original, uncorrupted form. Their intent was not a Nobel Prize, academic acclaim, or endless philosophical discourse; the goal of these Kabbalists was to bring simple happiness, peace, and fulfillment to all humanity.

PLEASE BE WARNED

There remains in effect a single warning, a strict prohibition concerning the wisdom and the lessons of Kabbalah. This warning dates from the second century and it is the first of 14 Spiritual Principles that will be presented in this book:

DON'T BELIEVE A WORD OF WHAT YOU READ!

It's been said that Kabbalah can address and answer all the age-old questions, including these:

— Is there a God?

— Why is life so filled with chaos and pain?

— Why are we here at all?

— How can I achieve uninterrupted fulfillment in my life?

Some say that Kabbalah is not just the light at the end of the tunnel, but the *Light that burns away and removes the tunnel itself*, opening up whole new dimensions of meaning and awareness.

Kabbalah can tell us many things: How and why the world began; Why we keep reverting back to our old negative habits; Why we keep avoiding activities we know are good and beneficial to our lives; How to instill meaning and spiritual power into every waking moment.

These are impressive statements—but don't believe them. Not one word. Not for one second. In fact, it's a principle of Kabbalah not to believe anything you read or hear. Because the very idea of belief implies a residue of doubt, but knowing leaves no trace of skepticism. It means certainty. Complete conviction. In your gut. In your heart. In your soul.

So please test each lesson of this book. Apply these principles to your life. Live the lessons, and see if your life gets better. Breathe the lessons, and see if the "air" gets cleaner. Much sacrifice and suffering has taken place so that in our day a book like this can reach you and the rest of humanity. It is therefore important for all of us to heed the Kabbalistic precept that states, "No coercion in spirituality."

In other words, the intent of this book is not to preach, but rather to humbly teach! For that reason, do not accept these lessons blindly. There must be tangible results in your direct experience. When that happens, you will feel the truth of Kabbalah in your body and soul, and you will come to know the wisdom of the sages in your heart.

THE LANGUAGE OF ANALOGY

Power of Kabbalah is a book that's lighthearted and profoundly serious at once. When you read these chapters in the same spirit, you'll find fun and insight at the same time. Wisdom doesn't have to be complex, humdrum, and heavy. In Kabbalah, after all, wisdom is called the Light!

MISCONCEPTIONS ABOUT KABBALAH

*Those who danced were thought to be quite
insane by those who could not hear the music.*
— *Angela Monet*

In ancient times, the word, "Kabbalah," struck fear into the hearts of most religious leaders. Shrouded in secrecy and centuries ahead of its time in its speculations, Kabbalah became subject to false rumors and suspicions: Imagine yourself trying to explain the concept of a telephone or the Internet to people of the 15th or 16th centuries. You'd be branded as a mystic, and Kabbalah was called mysticism for that very reason. But what was once considered mysticism is now called science—as the writer Arthur C. Clarke put it, "*Any sufficiently advanced technology is indistinguishable from magic.*"

Kabbalah was and continues to be the original technology of life. It's the science of the soul and the physics (and metaphysics) of fulfillment. And because it was an innovative philosophy that appeared on the scene thousands of years before its time, it was engulfed by misunderstanding—including the warning that Kabbalah can make you crazy.

That's right! Long ago it was thought that the study of Kabbalah could drive one to madness, to which this book responds...

LET'S GET CRAZY!

If our society considers heart attacks, panic attacks, ozone cracks, homicide, genocide, suicide, airline crashes, stock market crashes, ethnic clashes, high school shootings, religious feuding, recession, depression, therapy sessions, family welfare, chemical warfare, claustrophobia, xenophobia, unemployment, missile deployments, persecution, executions, political payoffs, massive layoffs, tabloids, steroids, illness, loneliness, earthquakes, poisoned lakes, along with disease, drug addiction, and death to be perfectly sane—then yes, Kabbalah can make you crazy!

So are you ready to get a little bit loony? Wonderful!

PART ONE

WHO ARE WE?

THE MAKEUP OF HUMANITY

Who are we? What is our basic makeup? What is our substance, our essence, the core of our being? What's the essential element that we are made of? Did you ever stop and contemplate that question? Kabbalah defines us in one simple word:

DESIRE!

DESIRE IN MOTION

When Kabbalah uses the word, *desire,* to define us, it is not a metaphor. Desire is truly our essential quality. Desire is the stuff that we are made of. It is our essence. Desire is what drives us. It's what makes us tick. We are all desires on foot, constantly seeking to fulfill our own cravings. Your heart beats, your blood flows, your body moves solely because there is a *desire* seeking to be fulfilled. Kabbalist Rav Ashlag once wrote that humans would not twitch a single finger if not for *some inner desire.*

DESIRE AND DIVERSITY

At heart, our individual human desires give us our separate identities:

Some people desire sexual fulfillment. Some desire intellectual fulfillment. Some want religious fulfillment. Others seek the material kind. Some of us desire fame. Some seek enlightenment. Some of us seek travel and adventure. Others seek solitude.

According to Kabbalah, human desires operate on three levels:

LEVEL ONE

These desires are rooted in animal lust. A person's needs, wants, and learned behaviors exist only to gratify these primal urges. People at Level One may make use of rational thought, as all human beings do, but it is for the purpose of serving their animal desire. "A slave is never more than its master," states Kabbalist Rav Ashlag.

LEVEL TWO

These desires are directed toward fulfilling drives not found in the animal kingdom, such as honor, power, prestige, and dominion over others. The needs, and consequently, the thoughts and actions of these people are directed only to gratifying these desires to the fullest extent.

LEVEL THREE

Still other desires are directed mainly toward rational matters. They are oriented toward gratifying an intellectually driven desire to its fullest.

"These three types of desire," Rav Ashlag states, "are found in all members of the human race; however, they are blended in each individual in different proportions, and it is this that makes for the differences that exist between one man and another."

A VESSEL

In the language of Kabbalah, desire is referred to as a Vessel. A Vessel is like an empty cup that seeks to be filled. Unlike an empty physical cup, however, the Vessel of our desires is not founded upon anything material. For instance, remember the time you consumed a sizzling steak to the point of nearly bursting the buttons on your shirt? You couldn't eat another morsel. But then the dessert cart was wheeled over to your table and you were staring at a tray of decadent sweets. Though your stomach was full, your new desire for something sweet managed to make a little room. A space was miraculously created and, the next thing you knew, you were gobbling up Black Forest cake. There is no limit to our desire. And there is not one activity in this world that is not founded upon some inner urge, large or small, yearning to be fulfilled. It's as though we have no free will in the matter. We live life on autopilot, driven by the constant need to nourish all the longings that linger in our hearts.

THE OBJECTIVE OF OUR DESIRE

The primary objective of our desire is *uninterrupted happiness.* In fact, desiring continual happiness is the one unifying link of all humanity. You don't have to convince a criminal, a lawyer, a construction worker, a CEO, a wicked person, a kind person, an atheist, a pious person, a mogul, or a pauper to want happiness. It is our very essence. A scientist might desire truth and understanding. Perhaps a politician desires influence and standing in the community. A child generally desires play and pleasure. A comic might desire laughter, love, and acceptance. A CEO usually desires financial achievement and power. A factory worker probably desires a vacation and peace of mind. Maybe a scholar desires knowledge and acclaim. In truth, all the objects of our desires are really just different packages of fulfillment. These various containers of contentment are what set us in motion and shape our lives.

Kabbalah sums up all these different packages of fulfillment into one word...

LIGHT!

The term *Light* is merely a code word, a metaphor created by the ancient Kabbalists to convey the broad spectrum of fulfillment for which human beings long. Did you ever gaze at a beam of sunlight after a cool rain on a hot summer day? When the shaft of sunlight strikes a droplet of water in the air, the light refracts into the seven colors of the rainbow. Just as this single ray of sunlight includes all the colors of the spectrum, the word *Light* suggests all the "colors" of joy that people seek in their lives.

But Light is not defined solely as happiness and joy. Kabbalistically, Light denotes *unending* happiness, *constant* joy. It's the difference between pleasure and fulfillment. We don't really want a momentary pleasurable high. Our deepest desires are not limited to 15 minutes of fame. Or a temporary rush from closing a business deal. Or a short-term high from drugs. Or temporary relief from a painkiller. We don't want to be liked by our peers for just a limited period of time. We don't want to be healthy for just half of our lives. We don't want passionate sexual relations with our spouses for just the first two months of a relationship. We want our desires to be constantly filled. This constant fulfillment is defined as Light.

Light also includes the force that we call *intuition*. The bond that holds a relationship together and keeps it strong. The magic that attracts the right people and right opportunities to our lives. The energy that heals a cut on an arm. The force that activates our immune systems. The inner spirit that arouses hope within us. The fuel that generates our self-motivation. The enduring happiness and constant flow of enthusiasm for living. All of this, and a whole lot more, is what Kabbalah defines as Light.

THE ROOT OF OUR UNHAPPINESS

The fact that our desires are not constantly infused with Light is the foundation of our unhappiness and anxiety. If there is joy in an area of our lives for five years, it means there was only enough Light in the "tank" to last for those five years. Running out of Light—or rather, disconnecting from Light—is what made us unhappy. The more Light we have in our lives, the longer our desires remain fulfilled and the happier we are. There is also a lingering deep-seated fear that our happiness will eventually end. When we find ourselves in a rare state of contentment and serenity, we have a negative tendency to believe it's too good to be true. We worry about tomorrow. And the moment these doubts creep in, the instant we begin to worry about how long it will last, we just ran out of Light. We lost the connection. Light is therefore also defined as the comfort, security, and peace of mind of knowing that happiness will still be with us tomorrow. When we are confident in the Light, there is no fear, anxiety, or insecurity about the future.

ULTIMATE DESIRE

The Kabbalists tell us that a human being's ultimate desire is desire for Light. Moreover, the Kabbalists tell us that this Light is *everywhere*. It is the most common substance in our universe. It fills the cosmos and saturates our reality. This Light is infinite, boundless, always ready to fulfill more than we can imagine. Which leads us to this compelling question:

If people are the essence of desire, and the universe is flooded with Light, what's standing in the way of our everlasting happiness?

ANSWER: A CURTAIN.

TWO SIDES OF THE CURTAIN: THE 1 PERCENT AND THE 99 PERCENT

According to Kabbalah, there is an actual *curtain* that divides our reality into two realms, which Kabbalah identifies as the *1 percent* and the *99 percent*. The one percent realm encompasses our physical world. But this is only a tiny fraction of all creation. It is only what we perceive with our five senses, what we can smell, taste, touch, see, and hear.

On the other side of the curtain lies the 99 percent, which encompasses the vast majority of reality.

In the 1 percent realm, life has an annoying habit of catching us off guard. We are afflicted with something called the *Suddenly Syndrome*:

- *Suddenly*, there was a problem in the business.

- He had a *sudden* heart attack!

- All of a *sudden*, he walked out on her.

- *Suddenly*, we're short of cash.

- There was a *sudden* problem in the relationship.

37

- He dropped dead *suddenly*.

- The deal *suddenly* fell through.

- She *suddenly* changed her mind.

- The doctors *suddenly* found a lump.

- The accident happened so *suddenly*.

- The good times *suddenly* ended.

- All of a *sudden*, the car came out of nowhere.

- We were so happy and then all of a *sudden*…

But is there really such a thing as "suddenly"? Kabbalah says no. Absolutely not! There is always a concealed, unseen cause that preceded any "sudden" event. Did you ever wake up one morning to suddenly find a full-grown oak tree standing tall on your front lawn? Of course not. Somewhere in the past a seed was carefully planted. When a nasty problem suddenly pops up and cuts off the flow of happiness that was fulfilling a particular desire of yours, it was not just some random, chaotic event, according to Kabbalah. There exists a deeper cause. Somewhere in the past, a seed was planted.

CHAOS THEORY

The *Suddenly Syndrome* originates in our inability to see through the illusions of our lives in the 1 percent realm. We cannot see beyond the immediate turmoil in order to grasp the big picture. We cannot see the other side of the curtain where the larger reality resides. Meteorologists faced this same problem when trying to predict weather. Storms and other fluctuations in the atmospheric conditions occurred without warning. They concluded that weather was a chaotic, nonlinear, and random sequence of events. Further scientific study has revealed a mysterious order concealed within the chaos. Science calls this phenomenon the *Butterfly Effect*.

THE BUTTERFLY EFFECT

Incredible as it seems, the tiny turbulence created by a butterfly flapping its wings in Tokyo can eventually amplify into a tornado in Kansas. A person slamming a car door in Iowa can therefore influence the weather in Brazil. Everything is connected on a deeper level of reality. Weather only appears random to meteorologists because they are unable to perceive and measure all the millions of influences that contributed to a stormy day—such as flapping butterflies and slamming doors. Kabbalah revealed this concept centuries ago. Our lives, no matter how chaotic they may appear, contain order hidden within.

The problem is that a curtain limits our ability to spot all those tiny butterflies blowing the winds of chaos into our personal lives. Nevertheless, all the storms and tornadoes whipping through our lives have their own unseen causes hiding behind the curtain. We observe effects but not the cause level of reality. We are blind to the remaining 99 percent. So here we are, in touch with a microscopic portion of reality as we desperately search it for fulfillment of our deepest desires. Some of us turn to science, some to traditional religion, some to drugs. Some pursue wealth and power. But the inner void remains. We feel insignificant, helpless, and out of control, starving for spiritual sustenance and positive change.

Will we remain prisoners of this 1 percent realm and miss out on 99 percent of reality? Will we be doomed to chaos and darkness? Must the curtain remain up forever?

Not by a long shot.

THE 99 PERCENT WORLD

A physicist had a horseshoe hanging on the door of his laboratory. His colleagues were surprised and asked whether he believed that it would bring luck to his experiments. He answered, "No, I don't believe in superstitions. But I have been told that it works even if you don't believe in it."

— From A Random Walk in Science, by R. L. Weber

The familiar reality is the 1 percent world in which we live, yet there is another side to this curtain—the 99 percent—and it is ultimately far more important. According to Kabbalah, the 99 percent realm is the source of all lasting fulfillment. All knowledge, wisdom, and joy dwell in this realm. This is the domain the Kabbalists call Light. Whenever we experience joy, we've made contact with this realm through some action that has taken place in the 1 percent realm. It may be from experience of a hug from your child or that you just closed a significant business deal. Wherever it came from, the joy you feel flows from the 99 percent.

NOTHING NEW UNDER THE SUN

Before Thomas Edison, civilization lived pretty much in the dark compared to the 24 hour, neon–lit, fluorescent–glowing, halogen–burning world of today. Did Edison really invent something new when he produced the first light bulb? Or did the information on how to build a light bulb already exist?

In other words, if someone had had the same information and materials for building a light bulb 100 years before Edison, couldn't the light have been switched on much sooner?

Did Albert Einstein actually discover something new with his Theory of Relativity, or was it always there?

Did Isaac Newton invent gravity when he discovered its properties, or did gravity always exist?

Edison, Einstein, and Newton merely *revealed* something that already existed. So where was all this information hiding before these great minds uncovered it? The answer, according to Kabbalah, is in *the 99 percent world.*

TIMELESS SYMPHONY

Mozart said that he was able to conceive entire symphonies in his mind before he wrote a single note. When he mentally experienced an hour of music in just a split second, Mozart felt that he was tapping into another reality. He was transcending the laws of time and space, and entering a spiritual dimension. Similarly, great scientific minds of the past believed that spiritual insight played a role in their achievements. Today, scientists are beginning to recognize that the spiritual dimension can be a source of great insight and inspiration.

Consider the case of Russian chemist Dmitry Mendeleyev, who had an unusual dream in 1869. Said Mendeleyev:

I saw in a dream a table where all the elements fell into place as required. Awakening, I immediately wrote it down on a piece of paper.

Mendeleyev's dream resulted in the Periodic Table of the Elements that we all learned about in our high school chemistry classes.

Insulin, used to treat diabetes, was discovered by Canadian physician Sir Frederick Banting. Banting had a dream that hinted at a method for extracting the substance from a nonhuman pancreas. Banting won the Nobel Prize and was eventually knighted for his discoveries.

American inventor Elias Howe dreamt about being chased by cannibals with spears. While the natives were waving their spears, he noticed the shafts all had tiny holes in them. The spears were also bobbing up and down. After this dream, Howe was finally able to complete his invention of the automatic sewing machine. He realized that he had to move the eye of the needle to the bottom of the needle instead of placing it at the top.

Renowned scientist Niels Bohr claimed that he dreamt of sitting on the sun with all the planets hissing around on tiny cords. Thereafter, Bohr developed the model of the atom.

Robert Louis Stevenson reported that the theme for his classic story, *Dr. Jekyll and Mr. Hyde,* originated in a dream, as did much of his best work.

In his book, *Shadows of the Mind*, eminent physicist Roger Penrose wrote:

According to Plato, mathematical concepts

and mathematical truths inhabit an actual world of their own that is timeless and without physical location. Plato's world is an ideal world of perfect forms, distinct from the physical world, but in terms of which the physical world must be understood.

THE MOMENT OF CONNECTION

Plato called a connection to the 99 percent, "divine madness."

Famed philosopher Nicholas of Cusa called it "divine revelation" or *docta ignorantia*.

Mozart described it as "a rush."

Philosopher E. Husserl called it "pure intuition" and "intuition."

Our mothers called it "a mother's intuition."

Your Aunt Rose termed it her "sixth sense."

Successful businesspeople call it a "gut instinct."

A BRIEF SUMMARY OF THE 1 PERCENT

The 1 percent reality is the world of our five senses. It is a realm of chaos in which:

- We react to external events.

- Fulfillment is temporary and fleeting.

- Effects, symptoms, and reactions preoccupy us.

- We are victims who apparently suffer because of other people's actions and external circumstances.

- There seems to be no hope for bringing about permanent, positive change because any change that occurs is temporary and therefore illusory.

- The majority of our desires remain unfulfilled.

Murphy's Law governs the realm of the 1 percent. Everything that can possibly go wrong *will* go wrong. Even when things go well, we know they'll change, for we live in an endless cycle of up and down.

A BRIEF SUMMARY OF THE 99 PERCENT

The 99 percent reality lies beyond human perception. It is:

- A world of absolute order, perfection, and spiritual Light.

- A realm of action rather than reaction to external events.

- The source, the seed, and the hidden origin of the physical world.

- A world of total fulfillment, infinite knowledge, and endless joy.

- A dimension in which we can initiate positive, lasting change, permanent change that also manifests in our 1 percent world.

There is *no trace* of Murphy's Law in the realm of the 99 percent!

This leads us to our Second Kabbalistic Principle:

Two Basic Realities Exist:

Our One Percent World of Darkness and the Ninety-nine Percent Realm of Light!

THE PROBLEM

There is one nagging obstacle—it's our inability to control the moments of connection to the 99 percent realm. Accessing this dimension of Light is accidental and haphazard at best. Kabbalist Rav Berg describes the 99 percent reality as dancing on the edge of consciousness, like an enchanting dream that cannot quite be remembered. Moments before waking, there is a crucial instant when only a loose thread connects the dreamer to the dream. The harder the dreamer pulls on that delicate strand, the more quickly the fabric of the dream unravels and disappears. Try as he or she might to reattach the thread, the dream fades and the dreamer must become resolved to a waking reality immensely inferior to that of the dream.

Imagine if we could access this realm at will! We would gain the ability to control all the events in our lives. Instead of dealing with symptoms and effects, we could discover the hidden forces behind chaotic circumstances and maddening events that "suddenly" end our happiness, leaving our deepest desires unfulfilled.

Think of it this way. If you alter a branch of a tree, you change the branch. Modify a leaf, and you change the leaf. However, if you can manipulate the genetic information inside the seed, you can affect the entire tree—branches, leaves, fruit, the whole shebang.

The realm of the 99 percent is the DNA level of reality: The seed. The root. The cause of all causes.

CHASING OUR OWN SHADOWS

Consider the following analogy: Your shadow on a sidewalk represents a severely limited version of your true self. Your shadow does not reflect the skin, hair, blood, bones, emotions, imagination, feelings, or desires that define you as an individual. It is merely a two-dimensional reflection of your three-dimensional reality. In this example, the shadow corresponds to the 1 percent world. Your true self corresponds to the dimension that lies beyond the five senses—that is, to the 99 percent. Could you move someone's arm simply by touching his or her shadow on the wall? It can't be done. You must touch the source, the actual arm, the 99 percent. You must move into a higher dimension to effect change: Move the actual arm, and the shadow responds automatically!

We have been conditioned to focus our awareness on the 1 percent realm of existence, which is akin to chasing our own shadows. Kabbalah says that won't cut it. It's an exercise in futility.

Here's a simple experiment you can try at home, that will exemplify the point. Get a piece of paper and a pencil, then write down your top five responses to the following question:

What does a human being truly desire from life?

THE TOP TEN LIST

When this question was asked to tens of thousands of people learning Kabbalah over the years, the following items turned up most frequently:

- Personal Fulfillment

- Peace of Mind

- Relief from Fear and Anxiety

- Financial Security

- Contentment

- Love

- Freedom

- Control

- Wisdom

- Happiness

- Health

Chances are, your list has something in common with this top ten list. Notice that not one of these items can be measured or weighed on a scale or held in our hands. We cannot physically locate any of these items on a map or reach them by geographically defining their coordinates. Interestingly, none of the things that we most want to receive from life is of a physical nature. Nothing on our list is found in the material 1 percent realm. Everything we genuinely desire is of an ethereal nature found only in the 99 percent reality.

Thus, our Third Spiritual Principle states:

Everything that a human being truly desires from life is spiritual Light!

So what do we do throughout our lives? We chase physical possessions in our pursuit of happiness. To see how this principle operates, let's look at something that would seem to be a very tangible asset: Money. Cold, hard cash. Consider an individual with a net worth of $20 million who loses $15 million overnight in a stock market crash. Compare that to a person with a net worth of $20,000 who suddenly earns $80,000 from a stock that just went through the roof. Which one goes to bed with greater financial peace of mind and a stronger sense of security? The one who still has $5 million, or the one with only a small fraction of that amount?

According to Kabbalah, material objects are not what we're really seeking in life. What we're really searching for is the spiritual energy that pervades the 99 percent world.

THE REASON FOR OUR DISCONTENT

We find ourselves unhappy, unfulfilled, discontent, sad, depressed, miserable, or anxious when our desires seem to be ignored by the universe. It's usually some form of chaos that precipitates our unfulfilled longings. Ill health. Financial adversity. Problems in the marriage. Social pressures. All this turmoil occurs when we disconnect ourselves, knowingly or unknowingly, from the 99 percent realm. When, however, we learn how to connect to this realm, we can control the events in our lives. We can prevent and eradicate the chaos that causes our unhappiness. We can turn on the Light and vanquish the darkness.

Contact with the 99 percent realm is the secret key to fulfillment in life. But it's not easy to do. That's why the ancient spiritual masters of Kabbalah gave us the tools and methods for reaching *beyond* our everyday lives. In the pages that follow, we'll explore and explain these tools in great detail.

IT MAKES YOU WONDER...

- Why do chaos, suffering, pain, and disease exist if there is another world of order and happiness?

- Why are there even such things as 1 percent and 99 percent realms?

- Who constructed reality in that way? And for what reason?

- Why is it that other spiritual systems teach us wisdom, but life still never really changes?

- Why are our desires and the fulfillment we seek separated by some unseen curtain?

- How do we inadvertently disconnect ourselves from the 99 percent realm?

- Where do our desires spring from?

- Why do they bother to exist?

- And finally, who hung up the curtain?

THE TASTE OF TIME

A tribesman of the rain forest will not suddenly wake up tomorrow morning and crave a double cappuccino or a Big Mac. Desires do not spring up of their own volition; the taste must have been tasted before. You cannot have a passion to enjoy another viewing of *The Godfather*, for the umpteenth time, if you never knew of or experienced the film before. A heroin addict will go to almost any lengths to score another hit. An alcoholic will stop at almost nothing when the craving for a drink appears. The basis for these incessant drives is that the experience of drugs or alcohol is already in the blood. Moreover, people with addictions know that this urge *can* be fulfilled, the "high" can be reexperienced.

Isn't it interesting that, since the dawn of humanity, people have been unrelenting in their quest for eternal happiness? No matter how many wars, diseases, famines, depressions, and natural disasters knock us off our feet, we keeping picking ourselves back up again, ever determined in our quest for lasting comfort, unending joy, and permanent pleasure. It stands to reason that we must have experienced this 99 percent realm before. Somewhere in the recesses of our souls, we know it's possible to connect ourselves to this reality on a continuing basis. It is not just a blind and senseless pursuit.

MEMORIES

According to Kabbalah, the very stuff of which the human body is composed—the atoms in our blood, the electrons that spur the impulses in our brains, the chemicals that make up our tissues and our bones—have roots that extend far back *before* the origin of our physical universe. The myriad desires, urges, impulses, and cravings that pervade our minds have existed since *before* the dawn of time. Whatever longings are stirring in your heart at this very moment are in fact memories lingering in your soul, recollections ingrained into your very being.

The pursuit of happiness is not only inscribed into the Constitution as an inalienable right of U.S. citizenship; it is also present in the blueprint of our universe. It is the inherited birthright of humanity.

Remember: An old oak tree didn't just spring up accidentally on your front lawn, out of nowhere. There was a hidden seed. Similarly, there is a seed of our desires and of the fulfillment we so desperately seek. We will now identify this ancient seed, and discover the ultimate purpose of our "sudden" appearance on the front lawns of this world.

PART TWO

CREATION,
THE BIG BANG
AND THE
NATURE OF GOD

THE CAUSE OF ALL CAUSES

For countless centuries, questions surrounding the origins of the cosmos were contemplated by rabbis, priests, scientists, shamans, spiritualists, philosophers, and physicists. Today, the scientific establishment largely agrees that some 15 billion years ago, the physical universe exploded into existence in what is now called the Big Bang. But science stops right there, leaving the ultimate question dangling in the vacuum of space—*why did the Big Bang occur in the first place?* What caused it? And how does the Big Bang relate to life in the big city today? Why should we concern ourselves with something that took place 15 billion years ago when we can't even figure out what went wrong in the last 15 minutes?

Only the ancient Kabbalists dared to answer these fundamental questions of existence. They traveled to a place where no one else had ever ventured—to that mysterious moment *before* the Creation of our universe!

WISDOM AS LIGHT

The spiritual wisdom and concepts that will be revealed in the pages that follow are older than time itself. These are the secrets of all secrets concerning the origin of our souls. These are the mysteries of all mysteries. The benefit attached to learning about our origins extends beyond greater intellectual knowledge. There is a mystical dimension attached to understanding the root of our existence. There is a spiritual benefit that comes with grasping these pristine principles. This long-hidden wisdom, according to the most learned Kabbalists, is also the stuff and substance of spiritual Light itself. Each new notion planted in our minds opens up pathways and portals into the 99 percent through which positive energy fills our beings. Learning Kabbalah unleashes hidden potential, allowing us to see and perceive things we never saw before. The most brilliant minds in history, including Pythagoras, Plato, Sir Isaac Newton, and Gottfried Wilhelm Leibniz explored Kabbalah's hidden wisdom, and it influenced them in profound ways. Remember, Newton didn't actually invent gravity. Sir Isaac merely discovered what was already there. The goal in studying

Kabbalah and the mysteries of our origins is not just to become more knowledgeable, but also purer, more enlightened, and more fulfilled.

PULLING BACK THE CURTAIN

Today, with the acceptance of quantum mechanics, relativity, and other leading-edge scientific theories, it appears that science is at last catching up to Kabbalah. As we'll discover in the pages that follow, these scientific viewpoints bear striking similarities to the cosmological speculations of the ancient Kabbalists. One distinct difference remains, however: Whereas science limits its explorations to how the world works, Kabbalah asks the ultimate question, *Why?*

Why does the world exist as it does?

Why are we here?

Why is my life the way it is?

If you've ever stopped to ask yourself these questions when life presented you with difficult challenges, you have your reason *why* you should read this chapter.

We're now going to sneak a peek behind the curtain and discover what really lies on the other side of reality.

Ready to take a look? Here goes:

Before planet Earth...

Before the universe...

Before the Big Bang...

Before time itself...

Back to the cause of all causes...

Know that before the emanations were emanated and the created were created, the exalted and simple Light filled the entire existence, and there was no empty space whatsoever.

— Kabbalist R. Isaac Luria, 16th century

ENERGY

Before time even began, there was an infinite force of *Energy*. This force reached as far as forever, filling eternity, expanding into infinity beyond time, space, or motion. According to Kabbalah, this boundless Energy was the only reality. And the nature of this Energy was to endlessly *expand, impart, share, and give*. The essence and substance of this Energy was infinite fulfillment, boundless joy, and limitless enlightenment.

Everything we've ever desired, and much more, is included within it:

Fulfillment...

Peace of mind...

Contentment...

Love...

Freedom...

Wisdom...

Happiness!

Everything positive that goes against the force of chaos, whatever is the antithesis of suffering and pain, anything that generates fulfillment, pleasure, and passion...all of it was included within this boundless force of Energy. In Kabbalah, this ever-expanding Energy of giving and sharing is known as the *First Cause*.

TWO TO TANGO

The concept of giving and sharing requires two consenting parties. After all, if there's no one to share with, how can sharing happen? If there is no one willing to receive the gift, how can the gift be given?

Imagine an old lady on the corner of a busy intersection. A passerby attempts to help her cross the street safely. She politely refuses. He tries again. She still refuses, now somewhat annoyed at his insistence. Why is she annoyed? Because she has no desire to cross the street. She's merely standing at the intersection waiting for the bus to arrive.

Although our passerby wanted to give, giving was impossible because the old lady didn't have a desire to receive what he was offering.

There must be a recipient, a willing receiver, a desire to take possession of the offering, for sharing or giving to take place.

THE VESSEL

To fulfill its giving nature, the infinite force of Energy created a receiver—Kabbalah calls it a *Vessel*—with which to share its essence. Imagine a cup full of water. The water inside the cup corresponds to the Energy. The cup corresponds to the Vessel that receives and contains the Energy. The Vessel, however, was not a physical entity. Rather, it was a force, an intelligent, nonmaterial essence.

The nature of the Vessel was an infinite *Desire to Receive*. In other words, for every kind of fulfillment and joy the Energy radiated forth, there was a corresponding *Desire to Receive* by the Vessel. Because this Energy force embodied an infinite variety of fulfillment, the Vessel consisted of infinite *Desires to Receive*. In down-to-earth terms, if there was sexual energy radiating from this Energy force, then a lustful desire for sex was aroused in the Vessel. If a box of chocolates was included within this Energy, then a sweet tooth and a craving for chocolate were actualized within the Vessel.

Seeing that this Energy force is defined as the First Cause, the Vessel is appropriately defined as the

First Effect. So we now have an infinite Energy and an infinite Vessel. Cause and effect. Sharing and receiving.

GOD AND HUMANITY

Let's close the curtain for just a moment. You've probably figured out by now that the Vessel is our root, our seed, our origin, our source. In fact, all the souls of humanity, past and present, were present within the Vessel.

Throughout the ages, the infinite force of Energy has been called God, Master of the Universe, Divine Creator, and many other names. The ancient Kabbalists referred to this Energy force by the Hebrew word, *Or*. In English, *Or* means the Light.

• As sunlight instantly expands and illuminates a darkened room on this side of the curtain, the Light expands and illuminates eternity on the other side of the curtain.

• As a single ray of light contains all the colors of the rainbow, the Light contains all the *colors* of fulfillment.

This Light that shines so brightly behind the curtain is the source and substance of all the fulfillment that we seek. All of our activities are, in actuality, pursuit of the Light, which manifests in myriad ways: rewarding relationships, prosperous careers, personal accomplishments, rich family life, emotional contentment, financial security, knowledge and wisdom, and all other goals that we strive for in pursuit of happiness.

THE LIGHT

The Light is not God, but an Energy that comes from God. Consider sunlight. The photons that fall on the earth are not the source and essence of the fiery solar body that gives us life from a distance of 91 million miles. Similarly, the Light is not actually the Creator, but rather His positive attributes and spiritual energy that radiate from His core. In even simpler terms, just as we cannot touch the nuclear furnace that is our sun, the human mind cannot conceive the totality of God. It makes little sense, therefore, to ponder the origins of infinity, when we cannot truly grasp or behold the concept of infinity itself. It's enough to know that the Light's joy and infinite fulfillment will completely and absolutely fill *any* and *all* human desires.

THE STRUCTURE OF THE VESSEL

The infinite Vessel was composed of two aspects—a male and a female energy, like a single battery containing positive and negative poles.

Kabbalah teaches that these two energies in one Vessel are known by the code name *Adam and Eve*. Adam and Eve were not just two people in the Garden of Eden. Some 2,000 years ago, the master Kabbalist Rabbi Shimon bar Yochai said that whoever takes the Bible literally is a fool. (Don't forget, these were his words!)

Kabbalists understand that the entire Bible is a code. And like any complex code, it requires deciphering and deeper understanding.

In a sense, it's like music. Imagine trying to hear a song and feel the composer's emotions simply by looking at the sheet music. It won't work. You must hear the melody and listen to the lyrics to fully appreciate the song.

Kabbalah is the instrument of our universe playing out the song of Creation.

The Bible is the sheet music.

Science relies on similar ideas. A physicist would never depend on the appearance of a rock to learn the fundamental nature of its realty at the level of atoms, protons, electrons and neutrons. The Bible also has a *subatomic* level far beneath the surface level of the text. In fact, the principal reason for the hostility between science and religion, and why religion has failed to fulfill the desires of all people, is that we've been reading the Bible literally. We've remained in the Stone Age concerning its *subatomic* level. This subatomic level is called Kabbalah. Thus, we learn that the code term *Adam and Eve* actually pertains to the one Vessel—which is itself an infinite conscious force known as the *Desire to Receive*.

ONE ACT OF CREATION

The creation of the Vessel—that is, the *Desire to Receive*—is the only true creation that has ever occurred. That's it. No other entities were constructed. No other worlds were fabricated from scratch. The only thing that ever came into existence—*ex nihilo*—was the desire to receive all that the Light was offering.

This single act of creation occurred before the origin of our universe. Within this one act of creation, however, there exist countless complex phases, which the ancient Kabbalistic texts have made known through discourse, metaphor, parable, and other cryptic language. Study of these phases requires many years, so an abbreviated rendition will be presented here.

The Light's sharing of its essence with the Vessel led to a remarkable unity. In Kabbalistic terms, this profound unity is called...

THE ENDLESS WORLD

If we could actually perceive the Endless World while peeking behind the curtain, it would be impossible to distinguish between the Light and the Vessel.

Imagine carving a cup from a block of ice. Then imagine pouring water into this cup. The cup is the receiver—the Vessel. The water is the giver—the Light. Water fills the cup just as the Light fills the Vessel.

At their very essence, however, both the water and the cup are H_2O. One essence, but two forms. The concepts of sharing and receiving occur within the one realm of H_2O. One reality, but two intelligences.

The Endless World operates in similar fashion. It is total perfection—the Light sharing completely with the Vessel. The ultimate manifestation of sharing and receiving. Unity. Harmony. Infinite giving and receiving of fulfillment.

THE MILLION-DOLLAR QUESTION

So what happened?

Where is this Endless World?

How did we end up here, in this very problematic existence?

Why are we trapped on this side of the curtain where all is dark and dangerous?

If everything was unified and perfect in the Endless World, why are we reading this book in a world that is fractured and flawed?

If we are part of the Vessel, why do we experience so much pain?

Where is the Light, the endless joy, the permanent happiness?

THE NATURE OF GOD

Consider an empty glass. What happens when you fill it with hot water? The glass itself heats up. This is analogous to what took place in the Endless World. As the Light continued to fill the Vessel, attributes of the Light were passed on. We might even say that the Vessel inherited the nature of its Creator. This inherited nature is the power to *create* fulfillment, *share* fulfillment, and play an active and causal role in the ongoing process of Creation.

BIRTH OF A NEW DESIRE

The Vessel inherited the nature of the Light, therefore, a new desire arose within the Vessel. This new desire was a longing to express what might be called the DNA of the Creator. Specifically, the Vessel wanted:

- To be the *cause* of its own happiness.

- To be the *creator* of its own fulfillment.

- To *share* fulfillment.

- To *control* its own affairs.

Infinite fulfillment was the reason the Vessel was created in the first place. However, because the Vessel could not express its "Creator genes," the Vessel no longer experienced *infinite fulfillment*. There was a singular desire that remained unsatisfied and that was a big problem.

To find out what happens in this next phase of creation, let's close the curtain on the 99 percent realm and turn our attention to a Little League baseball game taking place on a sun-soaked field during a warm spring day.

FIELD OF DREAMS

Bobby is nine years old. He's the pitcher on his Little League softball team. If Bobby could have just one wish in the whole world today, it would be to pitch a ballgame that would fill his parents with pride and joy! Bobby is getting his chance today because his coach has selected him as the starting pitcher. The little boy doesn't disappoint; he throws a no-hitter and sets a record for most strikeouts in a game.

After the final out, Bobby's teammates storm the mound, hoist him upon their shoulders, and parade him around the field in wild celebration. Bobby locks eyes with his parents, who are now beaming with delight in the stands. The emotions felt by this nine-year-old boy are indescribable.

After the game, Bobby discovers something rather shocking. It seems his dad had made a prior arrangement with both coaches and both teams to throw the game for his son. It was Bobby's birthday and his dad wanted his son to feel great on this special day. The entire game was fixed. From the first pitch to the last out. The hugs and cheers from his teammates were all staged. All because Dad wanted his son to experience those joyous feelings of victory and accomplishment.

How does Bobby feel now? Think about it for a moment.

BREAD OF SHAME

Bread of Shame is Kabbalah's term for all those dreadful feelings that little Bobby is experiencing. It's an ancient Kabbalistic phrase expressing all the negative emotions that accompany unearned good fortune. A down-on-his-luck man who is forced to accept charity from others is said to eat Bread of Shame. He has a deep-seated desire to earn the money needed to buy his own bread. He desperately longs to be in a situation where he can feed and support himself.

THE VESSEL HAD IT ALL IN THE ENDLESS WORLD, EXCEPT FOR ONE THING:

The ability to earn and be the cause of its own fulfillment!

Bread of Shame thus prevented the Vessel from experiencing absolute happiness.

This situation was certainly not the intent or thought behind Creation.

There was only one option: *Remove Bread of Shame.*

But how?

THE DILEMMA

As long as the Vessel did no more than receive, it remained unhappy. So what could the Vessel do to remove those awful feelings known as Bread of Shame? Sharing was not an option, because there was nothing to share with. There was only Light and Vessel unified in the Endless World. Perhaps the Vessel could share with the Light? A commendable idea, but the Light had no desire to receive. The Light is itself an infinite sharing force of Energy.

The Solution:

The Vessel stopped receiving the Light.

The Vessel pushed back, resisted the Light, and said, "No more!"

At that very moment, a *spiritual detonation* occurred—one that still reverberates to this day. People of science have detected the cosmic echo of this explosion, and have dubbed it…the Big Bang!!!

RESISTANCE

The ancient Kabbalists called the Vessel's act of pushing back the Light, *Resistance*. This word will come up again, so please remember it. The moment the Vessel resisted the Light from filling it, the Light withdrew and created a vacated space. The Light constricted itself, creating a single point of darkness within the Endless World. The infinite had given birth to the finite.

THE BIG BANG

The idea that the ancient Kabbalists understood that a Big Bang explosion began our universe is intriguing, to say the least.

That Bang was actually confirmed by the NASA satellite COBE just a few years back. Newspapers and television newscasts around the world announced the discovery with great excitement. World-renowned physicist Stephen Hawking said it was the discovery of the century. Astrophysicist George Smoot said it was like "Looking at God." Actually, it was more like looking at the Vessel's first effort to remove Bread of Shame.

Science, focused on the *hows* of physical reality, lacks the means to understand the spiritual significance of *why* the Big Bang occurred. Still, it's interesting to compare how ancient Kabbalah and 20th century physics describe the beginnings of our universe. The similarities are remarkable.

MODERN SCIENCE

Approximately 15 billion years ago, before the universe came into existence, there was nothing. No time. No space. The universe began in a single point. This point was surrounded by nothingness. It had no width. No depth. No length. This speck contained the whole of space, time, and matter. The point erupted in an explosion of unimaginable force, expanding at the speed of light like a bubble. This energy eventually cooled and coalesced into matter—stars, galaxies, and planets.

KABBALAH

*From the writings of 16th century
Kabbalist, Rabbi Isaac Luria*

The universe was created out of nothingness from a single point of light. This nothingness is called the Endless World. The Endless World was filled with infinite Light. The Light was then resisted to a single point, creating primordial space. Beyond this point nothing is known. Therefore, the point is called the beginning. After the Resistance, the Endless World issued forth a ray of Light. This ray of Light then expanded rapidly. All matter emanated from that point.

BIRTH OF A UNIVERSE

By resisting the Light, the Vessel took a tiny *first step* toward removing Bread of Shame.

Like a loving parent who stands back to allow a child to fall so the child will eventually learn to walk, the Light withdrew the moment the Vessel said, "Thanks, but no thanks. I'd like to learn to create and share some Light on my own."

The Light gave the Vessel time and space in which to evolve its own divine nature.

The *time and space* given to the Vessel is our physical universe.

PART THREE

THE PUZZLE OF CREATION
AND THE THEORY
OF RELATIVITY

THE PUZZLEMAKER

There was once a kind, old Puzzlemaker who possessed magical powers. The Puzzlemaker's greatest pleasure came from creating enchanting picture puzzles for the children who lived in his neighborhood. These puzzles were no ordinary puzzles. They had magical properties—when the final piece was snapped into place, beams of light would radiate from the images, filling the children with joy. All they had to do was gaze at the picture. Nothing more. For the kids, it was better than eating 10,000 chocolate chip cookies and drinking 10,000 glasses of milk.

One fine day, the Puzzlemaker truly outdid himself. He painted his most spellbinding picture ever, using magical paints flecked with stardust and special brushes whose handles were encased in gold. The Puzzlemaker was so excited by his creation, he decided not to carve the picture into individual puzzle pieces. Instead, he wanted the children to experience all the magic immediately.

As he finished packaging the picture, a little boy walked into the shop hoping to find the

Puzzlemaker's latest creation. The Puzzlemaker excitedly handed over the package. The boy's bright-eyed smile suddenly disappeared. His face turned a little sad. Clearly, he was disappointed at something. "What's wrong?" the Puzzlemaker asked. The little boy explained that building and creating the puzzle was half the fun! The Puzzlemaker understood immediately. With as much love and care as he put into creating the original image, the Puzzlemaker cut and disassembled the picture. He then lovingly scattered the individual pieces into the box. He had given the children what they really wanted more than anything else—the joy and accomplishment of building the magical puzzle from scratch.

To provide the Vessel with the opportunity to create its own fulfillment, the Endless World was disassembled and transformed into a picture puzzle. By allowing the Vessel to reassemble the puzzle of Creation, we, the Vessel, become co-creators of our fulfillment and thus remove Bread of Shame.

A TEN-DIMENSIONAL CURTAIN

To conceal the blazing Light of the Endless World—and to create the tiny point into which our universe would be born—a series of ten curtains were erected. Each successive curtain further reduced the emanation of Light, gradually transforming its brilliance almost to darkness.

These ten curtains created ten distinct dimensions. In Hebrew, they are called the *Ten Sfirot*, or the Tree of Life.

THE TEN SFIROT

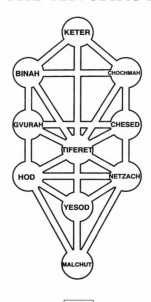

Keter, the top dimension, represents the highest level, closest to the Endless World. *Malchut*, located at the bottom, denotes the lowest level, our physical universe.

THE POWER OF DARKNESS

A burning candle emits no light against the backdrop of a brilliant sunlit day. But in a darkened football stadium, even a single candle is clearly visible. Similarly, the Vessel was incapable of creating and sharing in a realm already radiating Light. It was essential that an area of darkness come into being to transform us from passive *receivers* into beings who genuinely *earned* and created their Light and fulfillment. Therein lies the purpose of the curtains.

The only remnant of Light in our darkened universe is a "pilot light" that sustains our existence. This "pilot light" is the life force of humanity. This "pilot light" is the force that gives birth to stars, sustains suns, and sets everything in motion—from beating hearts to swirling galaxies to industrious anthills.

DISASSEMBLING THE PUZZLE

A puzzle can only be a puzzle if there is space separating the individual pieces and time given to reassemble it. The Endless World is a realm without time and space; therefore the Light had to create these concepts. This occurred automatically when the Light was hidden by the ten curtains. Dimming the Light meant obscuring its true attributes: If Light exists on one side of a curtain, darkness must materialize on the other side when a curtain blocks out the Light. Likewise, if timelessness is the reality on one side of a curtain, the illusion of time is created on the other side. If there is perfect order on one side of the curtain, chaos exists in the other dimension. If there is wholeness and exquisite unity on one side of the curtain then there is space and the laws of physics on the other side. If God is a blatant reality and truth on one side of the curtain, then Godlessness and atheism are the reality on the other side. Thus, in a sense, atheists would be correct in their viewpoint that there is no such thing as God. However, our uniquely human purpose in this world is to transcend our 1 percent realm and discover a higher truth, which is the subject of this book. Are you starting to get the picture? Welcome to our world of darkness!

But take heart, for in reality, the Light is still here. Cover a lamp with many layers of cloth and eventually a room becomes dark. Yet the lamp is shining brightly as ever. The intensity of light never changed. What changed was cloth covering the light. Kabbalah teaches us how to remove the layers of cloth one strip at a time—to reassemble the puzzle of Creation and bring ever more Light into our lives.

ADAM AND ATOM: PARTNERS IN CREATION

In a process whose description lies beyond the scope of this book, the one infinite Vessel broke into two distinct forces of spiritual energy: The male principle, called *Adam*, separated from the female principle, called *Eve*.

These two segments then shattered into countless pieces. These are the fragments of matter and energy that make up the cosmos, from atoms to zebras, from microbes to musicians. Everything is a portion of the original Vessel.

Adam had become *atom*. Or more precisely, Adam became the proton in an atom while Eve embodied the electron. These are the male and female energy principles that animate our universe.

Everyone's souls were part of the first, infinite, primordial Soul that shattered. Therefore, according to Kabbalah, *everything* in the universe is imbued with its own spark of Light, its own life force. Does this mean that even inanimate objects have souls? Does a rock have a soul? The answer is yes! The only difference between the soul of a rock and the soul of a rock star is the degree and intensity of their desire to receive Light.

The more Light an entity desires and receives, the greater its intelligence and self-awareness. A human being is more intelligent and self-aware than an ant, and an ant is more intelligent and self-aware than a rock.

LABOR CONTRACTIONS

At the precise moment of the Vessel's shattering, the Ten Sfirot underwent a sudden contraction in preparation for the birth of our universe.

Six of the ten dimensions enfolded into one and are known collectively as the Upper World.

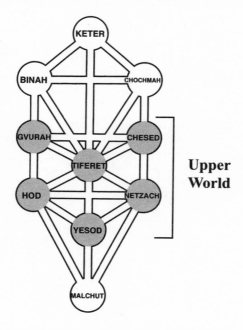

Upper World

This contraction, according to 12th century Kabbalist Moses ben Nachman, is the Kabbalistic secret behind the phrase, *Six days of Creation*. Why, after all, would an all–powerful Creator require any amount of time to create a universe? God should be able to whip up a universe in less than a nanosecond!

Kabbalist Moses ben Nachman agreed. Some 800 years ago, he explained that six days of Creation has nothing at all to do with the concept of time as we know it. It is a code for the uniting of the six dimensions into one.

In case you haven't been counting, four dimensions are still left out of the ten. These are the precursors to our three-dimensional universe, and to the fourth dimension of space-time.

SCIENCE CATCHES UP WITH KABBALAH

Two thousand years after the ancient Kabbalists revealed that reality exists in ten dimensions—and that six of those dimensions are compacted into one—physicists arrived at the same conclusions. This has come to be called *Superstring Theory*.

According to this theory, our universe is built of tiny vibrating loops. Different vibrations create different particles of matter, just as vibrations of a guitar string produce various notes of music.

Dr. Michio Kaku is an internationally recognized authority in theoretical physics and a leading proponent of Superstring Theory. In the journal *New Scientist*, Dr. Kaku wrote:

The Universe is a symphony of vibrating strings. And when strings move in ten-dimensional space-time, they warp the space-time surrounding them in precisely the way predicted by general relativity. Physicists retrieve our more familiar four-dimensional Universe by assuming that, during the Big Bang, six of the ten dimensions curled up (or "compactified") into a tiny ball, while the remaining four expanded explosively, giving us the Universe we see.

Dr. Kaku discussed the impact of this new (or old) idea on the scientific community. "To its supporters, this prediction that the Universe originally began in ten dimensions introduces a startling, new realm of breathtaking mathematics into the world of physics," Dr. Kaku wrote. "To its critics, it borders on science fiction."

Dr. Kaku, who wrote a best-selling book on superstrings entitled *Hyperspace*, was surprised by the intriguing similarities between Kabbalah and the Superstring Theory. "It's eerie," he said, "how the magic numbers of physics and the unified field theory are found in Kabbalah!"

A PRACTICAL SCIENCE

What does all this intriguing scientific-Kabbalistic babble mean to us on a practical level? How do the events in our lives relate to an explosion that occurred some 15 billion years ago? Why should we care if the universe has ten dimensions or 50 dimensions, for that matter? Many rabbis, scholars, and scientists have acknowledged that there are profound similarities between Kabbalah, the Big Bang, and Superstring Theory. But so what?! What's the relevance to our fears and phobias and desires for endless fulfillment? What's the connection to our unending urge for lasting happiness?

Therein lies the genius of Kabbalist Rav Ashlag. He synthesized these concepts, brought them down to our world, and shed a profound light on their relevance to human happiness.

As stated earlier, these six dimensions that lie just beyond our perception are known collectively as the Upper World. The Upper World is the 99 percent realm that we spoke about in earlier chapters (see the illustration on page 105).

1.   It is this 99 percent realm that we touch during those rare moments of clarity, rapture, mystical insight, expanded consciousness, epiphany, or the ability to pick the winning numbers in the lottery!

2. When Michael Jordan sank the winning shot to end the game and his career, the joy he experienced emerged from this realm.

3.   When your heart beats like a drum and passion overtakes you when you first catch glimpse of your soul mate, you are touching the 99 percent.

4. When you are lying on the beach with the sun splashing down on you and you haven't a care in the world, this almost supernatural serenity flows from worlds on high.

5.   Whenever you've felt pleasure, happiness, tranquility, inner peace, harmony, and the kind of confidence where you could conquer anything, you were touching one of the high levels in the Ten Sfirot.

6.   This is the realm that Plato wrote about — the timeless world of Ideas or Forms that exists

"beyond" the physical world of the five senses.

Remarkably, Sir Isaac Newton, the great scientist who has come to be seen as the very embodiment of the scientific method, concurred with this claim. Matt Goldish, in his book Judaism in the Theology of Sir Isaac Newton, quotes from one of Newton's theological manuscripts:

> Plato, traveling to Egypt when the Jews were numerous in that country, learnt there his metaphysical opinions about the superior beings and formal causes of all things, which he calls Ideas and which the Kabbalists call Sfirot...(MS. Yahuda, 15.7, p. 137v)

When we elevate ourselves and embrace this higher world, we bring lasting, positive change to our lives. Remember, move the arm that creates the shadow on the wall, and the shadow on the wall responds automatically.

How many times have you wondered, "*Where's God when I need Him most?*" How many times have we asked ourselves why it's so difficult to connect with the Creator? They key to connecting to the Creator and having our prayers answered is knowing how to connect ourselves to the Upper World known as the 99 percent realm. You will learn how to do that in the pages that follow.

THE THEORY OF REACTIVITY

Everyone thinks of changing the world, but no one thinks of changing himself.

— *Leo Tolstoy*

I wanted to change the world. But I have found that the only thing one can be sure of changing is oneself.

— *Aldous Huxley*

When we look into the realm of the 99 percent, we discover four key attributes of the Light that we inherited and need to express in our world in order to remove Bread of Shame.

They are:

1. **Being the Cause**

2. **Being a Creator**

3. **Being in Control**

4. **Sharing**

In our physical world, these four qualities merge into a single trait. My father, Kabbalist Rav Berg, elegantly expresses it in one word, directly relating to human behavior, PROACTIVE!

Further, all the traits of the Vessel—that is, of

humanity—can be expressed in the single word REACTIVE!

Reactive means:

1. **Being the Effect**

2. **Being a Created Entity**

3. **Being under the Control of Everything**

4. **Receiving**

In simplest terms, the mission of the Vessel is to transform itself from being a reactive force into a proactive force. Now, guess what?

This is the ultimate purpose of life;

The reason for our existence;

The meaning of our lives;

This is the way back home;

The path to endless fulfillment;

The secret to removing Bread of Shame;

And the true definition of the term *spiritual transformation*.

We have now unveiled the Fourth Principle of Kabbalah:

The purpose of life is spiritual transformation from a reactive being to a proactive being.

DECONSTRUCTING THE THEORY OF REACTIVITY

• **When we react to any external situations and events in our lives, we are merely an effect and not a cause; we are reactive, not proactive.**

• **Should we live our lives without any personal growth or change of nature, we are not creating new spiritual levels of existence for ourselves.**

• **When we allow outside forces to influence our feelings, positive or negative, we have surrendered control.**

• **When we exhibit egocentric or self-centered behavior, we are not sharing but instead receiving gratification for the ego.**

Reflect upon this well before proceeding to the next page!

A SPIRITUAL BIG BANG

Whenever we *react* in life, whether in anger or with pleasure, the energy we feel is a dangerous direct connection to the 99 percent. This is the Light the Vessel first received in the Endless World. This Light gives us a burst of energy. A rush of pleasure. A feeling of gratification. However, it was also this initial glow of Light that gave birth to Bread of Shame! *The Vessel rejected this Light because it was received in a reactive manner.*

Whenever we behave reactively, we are denying our inherited godly nature. Our soul then *replays* the original act of Resistance and stops the Light from flowing. A spiritual version of the Big Bang is reenacted. Metaphorically, another cloth is flung over the lamp. Life gets darker. And that's when the pleasure wears off. The thrill leaves us. The rush is gone. This is why we feel so down after we've reacted and exploded in anger toward our spouses. This is why we crash after experiencing a "high" from drugs. This is why our excitement eventually dissipates after buying a new car or new clothes. The gratification or pleasure we drew was not created through our own proactive efforts. Something external was responsible for our fulfillment.

In the same way, if someone pays us a compliment and it makes us feel better about ourselves, the *other person* is the cause and we are just the effect. Our happiness will be only temporary. Our soul is forced to reprise the act of Resistance and cut off the Light to prevent Bread of Shame. Darkness is the eventual result.

A SPIRITUAL ALTERNATIVE

There is another option available to us that prevents "spiritual big bangs" from taking place in our life. Kabbalah calls it Resistance, and it means stopping *all* of our reactive impulses through our choices.

Although this can be expressed in one short sentence, accomplishing it requires almost superhuman willpower and self-restraint. We'll find out why it's *easier said than done* shortly. Try the following exercise to deepen your understanding of Resistance and learn what transformation truly means.

THE $100,000 QUIZ

Scenario Number One: A hundred thousand dollars in small-denomination bills lies on top of a desk in a business. A man walks in and sees the money. He makes sure no one is watching, then scoops up the cash and flees like a bandit.

Scenario Number Two: A man walks in and sees the money. He begins shaking, fearful at the prospect of even touching the cash, let alone stealing it. He flees the building like a scared rabbit.

Scenario Number Three: A man walks in and sees the money. He checks to see that no one is looking. Then he scoops up the cash and begins to flee, but he stops. He agonizes for a moment and decides to return the money to the desk.

Scenario Number Four: A man walks in and sees the money. He takes it and places it inside a briefcase. He locks the briefcase and hands it over to the authorities for safekeeping. He leaves a note on the desk that informs whoever has misplaced a large sum of cash to contact him and he will direct that person to the authorities to retrieve the money.

Which scenario reveals more spiritual Light in our world? Which person expresses the most spiritual Light in his own life? Based upon all that we have learned, let's briefly examine each scenario to discover the answer.

Scenario Number One: In this case the man is governed by his reactive, instinctive desire to receive, which tells him to take the money and run. Reactive behavior produces no Light.

Scenario Number Two: This man is merely reacting to his instinctive desire to be frightened at even the thought of stealing the money. Reacting to his natural instinct produces no Light. The man enters the building and leaves it again with his nature unchanged.

Scenario Number Three: The man initially reacts to his desire to steal the cash. But then he *stops* his reaction. He shuts it down, proactively. Then, going against his initial instinct, he transforms his nature in this one instant and returns the money. His transformation from reactive to proactive reveals spiritual Light.

Scenario Number Four: Here the man merely

reacts to his instinctive desire to do the right thing. He was already in a proactive state of mind concerning stealing the money. No change of nature occurs. He remains the same person throughout the situation. Such behavior produces no Light.

The honorable man in this scenario can still reveal Light, however. After returning the money, he must not react to his ego, which tells him he is kind and virtuous. He must resist his desire to receive—which, in this case, means his desire to receive praise for his good deed. He must realize that the great opportunity is not the physical act of returning the money; it is keeping his good deed secret and rejecting self-praise.

THE LONG SUPERMARKET LINE OF LIFE

The next time you find yourself stuck in a long line at an ATM machine, traffic jam, or supermarket checkout counter, resist your urge to react. Do not get frustrated. Do not become impatient. Do not get angry. The line is there to test you, and to give you an opportunity *not* to react. But if you do react, the situation controls you. The situation becomes the cause and you the effect.

Always remember that the reason for not reacting to the long supermarket line, the crazy driver who cuts you off on the interstate, or your brother-in-law who irritates you to no end has nothing to do with being polite. Nor has it to do with good morals, ethics, or any other altruistic principle. It has to do with you, as in, *What's in it for you?*

Historically, morals have never led to peace and unity. Morality might be a noble concept, but it won't ever change the nature of the beast. Never has, never will. We are a species of receivers, as in *What's in it for me?* And that's okay. That was the Creator's intent.

In order to be motivated to take action, people must receive something in return. The purpose of Resistance is getting you closer to the Light so you can receive. So stop your reactive desire to constantly think about yourself—not because this is morally good, but because the transformation will serve your interests.

Each of us has the power to bring fulfillment to our lives by transforming our natures. When enough of us reach that level, the world will be overwhelmed with an unimaginable infusion of Light.

THE MOMENT OF TRANSFORMATION

We have two choices in life:

1. React to a situation, in which case our souls will eventually resist the Light, leaving us in the darkness of the 1 percent realm.

2. Proactively Resist our desire to react, thereby connecting ourselves to the 99 percent reality.

Option number two removes Bread of Shame, thus clearing the way for the Light to fill our lives in a particular circumstance. Put another way, the instant we resist a reaction, we have transformed a particular aspect our selves—which happens to be the purpose of our existence. We automatically link up with the 99 percent and the appropriate measure of Light radiates forth. Hence, our Fifth Spiritual Principle states:

In the moment of our transformation we make contact with the 99 percent realm!

THE TRANSFORMATION FORMULA

Changing reaction to proaction works like this:

1. **An obstacle occurs.**

2. **Realize your reaction—not the obstacle—is the real enemy.**

3. **Shut down your reactive system to allow the Light in.**

4. **Express your proactive nature.**

The moment of transformation takes place during steps three and four.

That is when you enjoin your soul to the luminous dimension of Light—the 99 percent realm.

APPLYING THE TRANSFORMATION FORMULA

Consider this scenario from life and watch how the formula works:

1. A difficult situation occurs. *Your friend blows up at you!*

2. Your emotional reaction. *You are upset, angry and hurt.*

3. Your behavioral reaction. *You yell back at your friend.*

ANALYZING THE TRANSFORMATION FORMULA

1. An obstacle occurs. *Your best friend blows up at you.*

2. Realize your *reaction* is the real enemy. *Your feelings of being upset, angry, and hurt are your real enemy—not your friend.*

3. Shut down your reactive system to allow the Light in. *Let go of all your emotional reactions. Instead of shouting back, take it all in. Even if you're not to blame, just let your friend vent. What matters* *is not who is right or wrong. What matters is your decision not to react.*

4. Express your proactive nature. *You are now in contact with the 99 percent. The emotions you will now feel and your next set of actions will be rooted in the Light. Automatically, positive feelings and behavior will come forth. You will see a surprising positive change in the external situation that was confronting you. Your friend will respond in a way you never dreamed possible. Or an enlightening piece of information concerning your relationship will suddenly come forth.*

All too often, our attention is focused on external circumstances. Someone we love hurts us. A business deal falls through. We disagree with someone else's opinion. Someone insults us. A colleague gets the promotion that we deserved. External events trigger reactions within us all day long. Instead of reacting, apply the formula. You'll see real miracles happen.

FURTHER DEFINING REACTIVE BEHAVIOR

Reactive behavior is founded upon the human Desire to Receive: This is the original desire that was created in the Endless World. Reactive behavior includes greed, selfishness, self-indulgence, ego, and the like. Reactive behavior is any reaction we have to external situations. This behavior can include anger, envy, overconfidence, low self-esteem, vindictiveness, and animosity. Take a moment and reflect upon these reactions. Recall the times when these emotions were provoked within you. Think about the situations that caused these feelings to come about.

In truth, 99 percent of our behavior is reactive. But that is by design. Remember, our essence is the desire to receive, to receive fulfillment.

Our consciousness is built on reactive, impulsive, instinctive desires. Rising above this consciousness constitutes genuine spiritual transformation.

Let's now examine how all these Kabbalistic concepts play themselves out in our real world.

PART FOUR

THE GAME, OUR OPPONENT,
AND THE ART OF
SPIRITUAL TRANSFORMATION

THE OLDEST GAME

Imagine 18 people gathered on a baseball diamond. All of them are endowed with tremendous athletic talent, on the level of Joe DiMaggio, Babe Ruth, Sandy Koufax, and Mark McGwire. They are given all the equipment necessary to stage a ballgame: bats, baseballs, mitts, and bases. We even throw in a wad of chewing gum.

But suppose they were missing one vital ingredient—the rules of the game. These 18 people have never heard of baseball and have absolutely no conception of what it is. What would happen if all these players were told to play the game called baseball, and they were not allowed to leave the field until they were as capable as World Series champs?

Imagine the chaos! Fighting. Arguing. Frustration. Quitting. Some players might make up their own rules. Although the players are endowed with the attributes of baseball stars, all they can produce is pandemonium.

According to Kabbalah, it doesn't matter how much talent we possess. Without the rules of the game, the result is chaos. Which brings us to a game a lot older than baseball, and a lot more mysterious. The rulebook for this most challenging game was recorded in an ancient Kabbalistic manuscript some 2,000 years ago. The book is called the *Zohar*, and it contains all the spiritual secrets governing the Game of Life.

According to the wisdom of the *Zohar*, each one of us is a potential Babe Ruth in the game of life. Each one of us is born into this world with enormous talent. But for most of us, this talent remains untapped—because we have been playing the game without really knowing how it's supposed to be played.

Kabbalah most definitely gives us rules, but without imposing constraints on our daily experience of the world. Instead, it presents a set of universal spiritual laws that liberate and empower us in body and soul. These laws are the 14 Spiritual Principles that are being presented throughout this book.

Before we can begin to understand Kabbalah's spiritual principles on a deeper level, however, we must first overcome an obstacle. Those talented people on the baseball diamond now have a rulebook, but suppose we blindfolded them before they took the field. Even though they know the rules, they can't see. So we've still got chaos!

According to Kabbalah, each of us comes into this world wearing a blindfold. Before we can continue to learn the rules of the game of life and truly act on them, we must first remove the blindfold and find out something rather important—*Who is our opponent?*

COUNTERINTELLIGENCE

Why does human nature seem so oriented toward self-destructive behavior? Why do we engage in activities that we know are bad for us, even when we don't want to? Why do we forsake what's good for us in favor of what's harmful? Why is greed more tempting and fun than generosity? Why is it so easy for us to get addicted to all things harmful? Why are good habits so difficult to develop?

Anger, fear, jealousy, laziness—all our negative and destructive behavioral traits—are like the force of gravity. No matter how hard we try to jump ten feet in the air, we can't. Negativity constantly pulls us down, no matter how committed we are to breaking free. It's built into our nature.

But we came to this world to change our nature! That's the deal that was struck in the Endless World. We, the Vessel, would no longer receive true and lasting fulfillment unless we removed Bread of Shame, unless we first transformed our reactive nature to proactive. But this task is extremely difficult. In fact, it's almost impossible. Why is human nature so balanced toward the negative?

THE OPPONENT

Real change is so hard because, as in every game, we are faced by an opponent in the game of Creation, one who constantly attempts to influence and control our behavior.

We've learned that, because of Bread of Shame, the Vessel wanted to earn the Light and be the cause of its own fulfillment. One way to gain an even deeper understanding of the Bread of Shame concept is to consider *the object of a game.*

In any athletic contest, the goal is to win. It doesn't matter if you're talking about the Los Angeles Lakers, Chicago Cubs, Miami Dolphins, New York Rangers, or a team playing in the Menomonee Falls Little League. If you ask someone what they're trying to accomplish, they will tell you it's to win the game. But is this really the goal?

Suppose a Kabbalist invoked a magic formula that allowed your team to win every single game. No matter what happened, you always won. Game after game. Season after season. The outcome was always predetermined, and there was always the same guaranteed victory.

What would that really be like? You'd quickly discover that the game had become extremely boring. The incentive would be lost.

So can we really say that winning is the ultimate goal? What we really want from a game is risk, challenge, and even the possibility of losing. More than winning, it's the test of our ability that makes it all worthwhile.

The concept of *losing* is what gives definition, existence, and meaning to the concept of *winning*. We "had it all" in the Endless World. Except for one thing: the ability to earn, deserve, and be the cause of the fulfillment that the Light bestowed upon us. So we rejected the Light in order to become *like* the Light—to become the creators of our own fulfillment.

We wanted the opportunity to play the game of Creation on our own, to risk losing season after season, lifetime after lifetime, for that one chance to win it all and bring home the trophy. Only then could we ever possibly know genuine feelings of accomplishment and happiness. Only then could we truly maximize our power to be proactive. Without testing us to the highest possible degree, the godlike proactive seed within us would never fully blossom.

Like spiritual Olympic athletes, we must train ourselves mentally and emotionally so that our divine-like nature can evolve and manifest. This training satisfies our need to *earn* and create the Light in our life and eradicate Bread of Shame.

THE COMPANY

A man builds a business from scratch into a multimillion-dollar corporation. After running the firm for 25 years, he decides to resign from his position as chief executive officer. He will become the chairman of the board, a position that is more honorary than hands-on.

Seeing that his daughter is blessed with talents equal to his own, the man awards his daughter 50 percent ownership in the firm as well as the position of CEO. But the promotion causes a problem for the young woman. Her father's blood, sweat, and tears—not her own—built the company, and although the father gave her the company out of love, admiration, and respect, the young woman feels as if she has received a handout.

The daughter would obviously love the half-ownership and the CEO position, but it has to be under the right conditions. So she devises a plan. The company employs thousands of people, so no one really knows who she is. She decides to apply for a job in the warehouse. She works hard for many months. After a while, she earns a promotion. Later, she earns another. She continues to work extremely hard over the years, and through countless hours of effort, determination, and her inherited head for business, she learns all facets of the operation as she climbs the ladder of success. Eventually, she works her way up to the top of the firm and becomes the president and CEO.

What's the difference between having stepped into ownership of the business and having risen through the ranks? The difference is, in her own mind, the daughter never really earned the ownership until she had worked her way up from the bottom.

The daughter knew that once she had achieved leadership through her own actions, she could enjoy everything her father had intended for her. Furthermore, only through this process could the father's goal also be fully realized.

It's important to understand that at no time during the daughter's climb up the corporate ladder could her father have interfered. If his daughter had experienced any pain or setback, or even if she had been fired, the father would have had to stand back and allow his daughter to work things out for herself, no matter how painful that might have been.

But the father had faith in his daughter. After all, he created her, and he knew that she was blessed with the same traits he himself had. He knew that once his daughter made it to the top, on her own merit, she would truly come to know and savor that wonderful feeling of achievement and fulfillment that comes with being an owner of the company.

In this story, the daughter is a metaphor for us— the Vessel—and the father is a metaphor for the Light. The Vessel needs to express its inherited proactive nature to remove Bread of Shame. To be proactive, we must first be reactive. And to be reactive, we need challenge. To make that transformation from reactive to proactive meaningful, worthwhile, and complete, we need a powerful opponent to test us.

Who is our opponent?

INTERNAL BATTLE

Two thousand years ago, the *Zohar* revealed our opponent. The *Zohar* even identified the various techniques, weapons, and strategies he uses. He is the unseen cause of chaos in the physical world and in the human spirit. His is the voice that whispers, "Eat the cake now. Start the diet again on Monday." It is he who arouses feelings of despair, pessimism, fear, anxiety, doubt, and uncertainty. He also foments overconfidence, ruthlessness, greed, jealousy, envy, anger, and vindictiveness. The opponent is the voice that says "Go and do it!" even though we know we shouldn't. The opponent is the voice that says "Don't bother with it!" even though we know we should.

And worst of all:

Even when we want to apply Resistance in our life and stop reactive behavior, our opponent shrewdly talks us out of it!

For instance:

You make a vow to start eating healthy foods—but the moment you see some junk food, the opponent coaxes you into putting it off another day.

You promise to spend more quality time with your family—but something compels you to put in a 60-hour work week.

You're driving and a passerby needs some assistance. Your initial thought is to stop and help—then your opponent convinces you that someone else will probably help. You rush off to your lunch engagement as the opponent rationalizes your unkind behavior the rest of the way.

You make a commitment to save a little bit of money each month and become more fiscally responsible—but each month the opponent convinces you to frivolously spend it all, justifying each expenditure in your mind.

You walk into a health food store and spend a ton of money on vitamins of every kind, genuinely committing yourself to a daily regiment of nutrients. Six months later, the bottles sit half full on your shelf. Next year the same thing happens when you find yourself back in the health food store. This time you promise yourself it will be different—but it isn't.

You're invited to an important family function. You know the right thing to do is to attend but a voice peeps up inside of you conjuring up a lame excuse. Instead, you stay home and watch a video.

A close friend confides in you, sharing a personal secret. You promise your friend (and yourself) not to divulge it to anyone. A few days later the opponent nudges the words right out of your mouth while you're gossiping with someone else. You actually watch yourself spill the beans, even though, as the words roll off your tongue, you know you shouldn't be doing it.

A dear friend moves into a nicer house than yours, or wears a new outfit or drives a sexy new car. You tell yourself to be happy for your friend but envy begins to raise its ugly head and you cannot control the jealousy stirring inside of you, even though you want to. Resentment and happiness for the other person battle for control over your emotions.

THE OPPONENT

Throughout history, religions, philosophers, and poets have given names to the opponent, including Lucifer, Beelzebub, Nobodaddy, Mr. Hyde, the Evil Inclination, the Dark Side, Darth Vader, the Dark Lord, the Beast, and the Wicked Witch of the West!

Whatever you choose to call it, the ancient Kabbalists said the opponent was real, very real. Though you cannot see this opponent with your eyes, it is as real as the invisible atoms in the air and as ubiquitous as the unseen force of gravity. So be warned. The opponent is watching you right now, as you read these words. His true name, as revealed by the ancient sages of Kabbalah, is שָׂטָן. In English, this translates to "the Satan"—with the accent on the second syllable (suh-táhn.)

The Satan is not the red-clad, double-horned demon who wields a mean pitchfork. These superstitions have only served to further conceal his true purpose and identity. His name is a code word for ego-driven, *reactive behavior* and he is the ultimate *master magician*. His deceptive talents are best summed up by a line from the film, *The Usual Suspects*:

> *The greatest trick the devil ever pulled was tricking humanity into believing that he doesn't really exist!*

The Satan has fooled us into believing that we are victims of outside forces and other people's actions. He has convinced us that our enemy is some other person instead of our own reactive nature. All the while, he hides in the shadows of our minds, lurking in the dark recesses of our beings so we never know he exists. He inflates our egos so we think we're brilliant and in control of our lives. All the doubts you have about his existence are his doing.

Most important, he blinds us to our own godly nature so that we don't even recognize our purpose in life. Think about it. How many people do you really know who look inward each day, trying to uproot their negative reactive traits? Yet that is the true purpose of our existence.

ALTERING OUR DNA

When the force called the Satan came into being, his appearance added another element to our *Desire to Receive*. It was as if our spiritual DNA had been altered, by adding a few more letters to the human genome. Those additional genetic letters are:

f.o.r. t.h.e. s.e.l.f. a.l.o.n.e.

Humanity was imbued with a *Desire to Receive for the Self Alone*. This additional "selfish gene" comes from the Satan. This is the singular root and motivating force behind humanity's reactive nature and our individual, impetuous, rash behavior. This is what makes the transformation from intolerant to tolerant so difficult.

Desire to Receive merely attracts and draws energy. Desire to Receive can draw material and spiritual possessions for ourselves or for the sake of sharing with others as well.

The Desire to Receive for the Self Alone, however, leaves not a scrap or morsel for anyone else. Like a black hole in deep space, this desire consumes everything within its vicinity, so that even spiritual Light itself cannot escape its power.

THE DIFFERENCE BETWEEN DESIRE TO RECEIVE AND DESIRE TO RECEIVE FOR THE SELF ALONE. ·

Desire to Receive is when you see another person's spiritual or physical possession, and a desire for the same possession is awakened within you. But the Desire to Receive for the Self Alone is when we attain a material possession, such as a car or a new designer outfit, and still we resent and begrudge our neighbor for buying the same item, even though it in no way diminishes our own possession. In other words, no one else should have but ourselves.

Here's how our opponent manipulates and controls our Desire to Receive for the Self Alone:

FIELDS OF BATTLE

We discover that the Universe shows evidence of a designing or controlling Power that has something in common with our own minds.

— *Sir James Jeans, physicist*

The battle against our opponent has been going on for a long time, yet it takes place on a very murky, ill-understood terrain. This is the landscape of the human mind. But before we can truly understand what this means for us, we must understand what the mind really is.

Suppose a primitive tribesman ventures out of the jungle with no knowledge of the modern world. He comes across a transistor radio playing music and looks at it in astonishment, believing that the box is the source of the music. He opens up the radio and accidentally pulls out the transistor. The music stops. This convinces him that the radio is the source. In fact, he thinks he has killed the poor little creature. Of course, we know that the source of the music is really some radio station broadcasting over the airwaves from many miles away...

Kabbalah teaches that our thoughts do not originate from the physical matter of the brain, just as music does not originate in the physical object of a radio. Instead, the brain is like an antenna, a receiving station that picks up a signal and then rebroadcasts it into the conscious mind.

During the 1950s, the brilliant neurosurgeon Wilder Penfield began extensive research into the mind–brain phenomenon. His goal was to explain how consciousness emerged from the physical matter of the brain. After 40 years of exhaustive study, Penfield admitted that he had failed. In *Mystery of the Mind* (Princeton University Press, 1975), a remarkable book detailing his decades of research, Penfield wrote:

> *The mind seems to act independently of the brain in the same sense that a programmer acts independently of his computer, however much he may depend upon the action of that computer for certain purposes.*

But who—or what—is that programmer?

RATINGS WAR

According to Kabbalah, two cosmic broadcasting stations—the Light and the Satan—send signals to our brains. It's a ratings battle for the audience of mind—a bigger and far greater ratings battle than the three major networks have ever seen!

If we could learn how to distinguish which thoughts are from the Light and which thoughts originate from the Satan, we could reclaim control of our lives.

A good starting point is this:

Any thought that is loud and crystal clear and urges us to react to a situation is the Satan.

Any thought that tells us that we are the architects of our own success and that we know better than the next guy is once again the voice of the Satan. The notion that our thoughts are chemical reactions in the brain is also the creation of our devious opponent.

If a thought is barely audible, a faint voice emanating from the recesses of our minds, it is the song of the Light. Or if there is a sudden flash of intuition, an impromptu inspiration, the broadcast is originating from the 99 percent realm.

These two frequencies on the airwaves of our minds express themselves in this way:

- **The Satan's thoughts manifest as our rational, logical minds and egos.**

- **The Light's signal manifests as intuition, dreams, and a faint quiet voice in the back of our minds.**

Usually, we are out of touch with our intuition. As a result, the Satan rules the airwaves of the mind and plays one particular hit song over and over again—the song called *Reaction!*

The secret to taking control of our lives is to cut off the Satan's signal. When we stop our reactive impulses, we literally turn off his broadcast.

When we succeed at this, even for a moment, the Light's signal is free to fill that space Our lives and our decisions are rooted in infinite wisdom. Automatically, we make the right choices. The right thoughts come to our minds. The perfect words are spoken. Proactive emotions appear. The best ideas come forth at once. We suddenly see the deep-seated wisdom in an opposing argument put forth by a colleague, friend or spouse.

But to prevent this from happening, our opponent has some cutting-edge strategies and some state-of-the art weaponry at his disposal.

TACTICS

The Satan's sole objective is to arouse our Desire to Receive for the Self Alone so that we disconnect from the Light. His major tactic is to simply push our reactive button all day long. When this button is pushed, we are consumed with negative thoughts, selfish impulses, and egocentric urges to fulfill our Desire to Receive for the Self Alone.

Thus, we lose touch with our essence, our soul. Another cloth is placed over the lamp. The curtain between the 1 percent and the 99 percent grows thicker. There is more darkness in our lives. From this darkness emerges chaos.

But when we proactively reenact the original Resistance—performed by the Vessel in the Endless World—by refusing to react, we are pulling an emergency lever that overrides the reactive button that the Satan pushed. This lever activates a shutoff valve that immediately cuts off the reactive emotions flooding our bodies. We are no longer reactive. We are proactive. We have made contact with our souls. And that is when the Light on the other side of the curtain shines into our lives.

WHAT'S UP IS DOWN, WHAT'S DOWN IS UP

Kabbalist Rabbi Yehuda Ashlag, the 20th century mystic, said that people usually perceive events to be exactly opposite of their true state of reality because of their limited view of reality.

To illustrate the point, he offered this simple thought experiment:

Imagine a person who has lived in total isolation since birth. He's never observed a living creature, either human or animal, in his entire life. Placed before him are a newborn hippopotamus and a newborn human baby. He observes the two. The baby obviously cannot take care of herself. She cannot crawl, let alone walk, and must be carried from place to place. She cannot communicate her needs clearly, or even feed herself. The baby doesn't fully perceive her surroundings. If a fire erupted near her, for instance, she would not even sense the danger. Basically, the newborn is helpless. But the baby hippo immediately perceives his environment. He knows to run from fire. He can feed himself. Within five minutes of birth, the newborn hippo can walk and swim.

What conclusion would our isolated observer

draw? Probably he would believe that the hippo was a more advanced creature than the baby. Rav Ashlag taught that the more advanced a creature is at the beginning of growth, the less developed it will be at the end. Conversely, the less advanced a creature is at the beginning of its development, the more advanced and evolved it will be by the end.

The same principle is at work in all areas of life. Opportunities that look promising at the outset turn out to be disasters, while seemingly hopeless situations unexpectedly prove to be blessings in disguise. We misjudge situations because we lack the ability to perceive both the short-term effects and the long-term outcome. We react to the moment.

Kabbalah teaches that, more times than not, the final outcome of any life process will be *the exact opposite* of the first impression. Our opponent tries to reverse this spiritual truth by inciting reactions to the present moment.

THE WEAPON OF TIME

Kabbalah defines time as the distance between cause and effect. Time is the separation between action and reaction. Time is the space between activity and repercussion, and the divide between crime and consequence. Yet time wreaks havoc in our lives. It creates the illusion of chaos when, in fact, there is a concealed order. Our five senses prevent us from seeing through the illusion of time.

It seems to us that the past is gone and the future is not yet here. Yet past and present are always with us. Two thousand years after the ancient Kabbalists revealed this concept, Einstein made similar assertions. It's only the limits of our consciousness that prevent us from perceiving yesterday—and tomorrow—right now!

But how can past, present, and future all exist at once? Imagine a 30-story building. We are now standing on the 15th floor, which represents the present moment. Floors 1 through 14 represent the increments of time that brought us to this moment. Floors 16 through 30 represent the future of our lives. What do we currently perceive with our five senses? Only the 15th floor. We cannot see the floors below, and we cannot see the floors above. Yet all the floors—that is, past, present, and future—exist as one unified whole: the entire 30-story building. And if we go outside the building and look at it from a distance, we can see all 30 stories at once!

That's a nice abstract concept to engage the mind, but what's the lesson for our lives? Who cares if time is really one? Who cares if tomorrow is here right now? We can't see tomorrow and we can't perceive yesterday, so what good does that information do us?

Good questions, and there is a lesson to be learned.

DELAY TACTICS

The illusion of time creates a distance between cause and effect. There is a space between behavior and consequence. There is a separation between our actions and their repercussions. This distance prevents us from perceiving the connections between the events of our lives. We might have planted a negative seed 30 years ago, but by the time it sprouted, we had forgotten the seed. Eventually, a tree (chaos) "suddenly" appeared out of nowhere. Yet nothing happens by chance. Everything can be traced to some seed planted in our past. Time just makes us forget the original causative action. Chaos appears to be sudden, because time has separated cause from effect.

THE TEST OF TIME

When we behave proactively, the Satan uses time against us to sabotage our accomplishments. Just as the chaos may be delayed, the Light due us may also be delayed. If we think we've been proactive, but find ourselves wondering when we'll get the Light, our adversary has won another round. It was just a devious delay tactic to incite us into reacting with doubt and disbelief. If we apply Resistance in a situation and our opponent throws a bit of time into the process, the spiritual Light owing might not shine immediately. Consider the delay an additional test to make sure our proactive response was genuine and deep. If we *react* to the delay, we lose.

Thus, time is further defined as the distance between good deeds and their dividends. Time is the space between Resistance and reward.

MANIPULATING TIME

The Satan also uses time in other ways. These include the concepts of "yesterday," "today," and "tomorrow."

>>**Yesterday:** All too often we find ourselves clinging to yesterday. We are prisoners to feelings of regret, vengeance, resentment, and other destructive emotions rooted in our past. We harbor these feelings and let them damage our lives in the present.

>>**Today:** Many of us find it tempting to run from the challenges and pressures of the present moment. So we procrastinate and put things off. We create false hopes about the future and live in denial about our current situation.

>>**Tomorrow:** We are filled with anxiety about *what will be*. We are frightened by the unknown future, terrified by tomorrow. We are not sure which decisions to make or what the outcomes of our choices will be. Fear and trepidation consume us.

All these feelings are *reactions*—because we have allowed time to control our lives.

THE WEAPON OF COMPLACENCY

Spirituality, according to Kabbalah, is not about trekking up a mountain to commune with God and nature while meditating alongside a clear stream as the birds sing the beauty of the world. That makes for a poetic scene, but it is not the purpose of our lives. Nor is divorcing ourselves from the physical world, secluding ourselves up on a mountaintop contemplating the majesty of nature. According to Kabbalah, these are not effective ways to achieve spiritual growth.

We came *down* from the mountain, so to speak, to enter the world of chaos, hardship, turmoil, and burden so we could confront the triggers that ignite reactions. Each trigger gives us the opportunity to transform our reactive behavior and remove the Bread of Shame. Transformation. That's how we rebuild the puzzle of creation. Like an old proverb says:

Smooth seas do not make skillful sailors.

In truth, our positive traits do not win us any points in life. Our wonderful characteristics and endearing qualities serve no practical purpose when it comes to arousing new levels of fulfillment and Light in our lives. Those traits are already in a proactive state. On the contrary, it is our negative characteristics and traits that give us the opportunity to affect a true transformation of character.

We came to this world to create positive change within ourselves and the world around us. Positive change will encounter resistance, conflict, and obstacles. We must embrace these difficult situations. A man can live in a small town, in a modest house with a white picket fence and a wonderful garden that he tends all day long. It's a good life, a tranquil life. At age 95, he passes on peacefully in his sleep. On the surface, it appears to be an ideal existence. But was this really his purpose on this planet? Was there any internal change in this man's life? Is he a different, more evolved spiritual being at age 95 than he was at 35 or 65?

Some people live 70 years as if it were one day. Some people live one day as if it were 70 years. The white picket fence, early retirement, the simple lifestyle—all of them lead to complacency. They can be weapons of our opponent. Our opponent will instill complacency within us to prevent us from making inner changes. Then, when it's too late, we realize life was empty and without meaning.

Even worse, some people go to their graves *without* realizing that their existence was empty. Always remember that our positive traits do not flip on the Light switch. The Light goes on only when we identify, uproot, and transform our reactive negative characteristics. *It is the degree of change in our natures that determines the measure of our fulfillment.*

THE WEAPON OF SPACE

What about all those people who actually seem to succeed with reactive, selfish behavior? Well, *seem* is the key word. Our actions in one area of life *seem* to have no relationship to consequences in other areas. This creates a marvelous illusion of space and separation, and the Satan takes full advantage of it. If you're a shark in business, the Satan has the power to redirect chaos toward your family life. If you are deceitful toward your spouse, the Satan can have the payback directed toward your business.

Ninety-nine percent of the time, our wants and desires are implanted by the Satan. Conversely, when the Light we generated by our proactive behavior in business materializes in our personal life, the Satan will keep us preoccupied with business. When the Light does not materialize as increased profits, we assume that our proactive behavior is not working. We will not notice that our children are suddenly feeling a stronger spiritual bond with us. The Satan limits our view and focuses our attention on situations that fuel our egos, so we fail to appreciate and receive the richness that life offers us.

THE WEAPON OF DISGUISE

One of the Satan's most potent weapons is the ability to confuse us. We feel sad and disoriented, angry and envious, and we never know who our real opponent is.

In the course of all the mergers and acquisitions, all the takeovers, deal cutting, wealth building, promotions, job changes, spousal fights, divorces, lawsuits, bypass operations, backstabbing, gossiping, bad-mouthing, rationalizing, justifying, and blaming, we think the opponents are our neighbors and friends whom we feel compelled to outdo with our cars, homes, clothes, and holidays. Or we think the opponent is our business competitor. Or the person at work who gets all the credit for the work we do. Or maybe the opponent is the whole rotten world, the whole corrupt system that has failed us and done us wrong. Maybe that's why our lives are so miserable.

But it isn't so. The Satan is a master magician. A master of disguise. The Satan projects himself onto other people so that you recognize all of your faults in others and see the enemy as *the other person*. In reality, you're playing against the Satan and don't even know it. You even doubt his existence right now, while reading a book on Kabbalah that plainly identifies him!

When someone wrongs you and you react, you lose. Even more remarkable, according to Kabbalah, *you deserved to be wronged by that person* because of a negative deed you committed previously in some area of your life. It is a critically important proactive behavior to remember this difficult truth the next time life gongs you over the head: Hence, the Sixth Kabbalistic Principle states:

Never—and that means never—lay blame on other people or external events.

UNMASKING OUR TRUE ADVERSARY

Here's a very powerful and practical technique to help you put this rule into action. Whenever someone does something really rotten to you, imagine that you can actually see the Satan whispering in that person's ear, causing all the negative behavior. See the person in front of you as a helpless puppet under the complete influence of the Satan. Recognize *him* as the culprit. Imagine him laughing at the two of you, as he tries to fan the flames of hatred and conflict between you.

How do you feel now? This should help alleviate your reactive emotions toward this person, putting you in a better frame of mind for the real spiritual work that begins when you look inward. Then you can see that the Satan was whispering in your ear, too. All your negative feelings were being provoked by his suggestions. He was helping you project all your negative traits onto the other person the whole time. In fact, you were able to recognize and react to negative traits in others only because you have them yourself.

RESISTANCE AND SHORT CIRCUITS

Kabbalist Rav Berg says that when Kabbalists speak of Light with a capital L, they are referring to the infinite Light of the Creator, the source of all our fulfillment. When Kabbalists speak of light with a lower case l, they are referring to sunlight or the light of a bulb. Both *light* and *Light* share similar characteristics concerning illumination.

Do you know how a light bulb works? Inside are three components:

1. a positive pole (+)

2. a negative pole (–)

3. a filament separating the (+) from the (–)

Of the three components, the filament is the most important. It acts as a resistor, pushing back the current flowing from the positive and preventing it from connecting directly with the negative. This resistance, or pushing back of energy, is the reason the bulb generates illumination. When the filament breaks, the positive connects directly with the negative and the bulb short-circuits. It bursts, producing a momentary flash of light. But then there is darkness. In other words, without resistance, there is no lasting Light.

THE LIGHT BULB METAPHOR APPLIED TO THE ENDLESS WORLD

★ The negative pole in a light bulb corresponds to the Vessel.

★ The positive pole corresponds to the Light.

★ The filament corresponds to the Vessel's act of Resistance, which caused the Big Bang.

At the moment the Vessel resisted and stopped receiving the Light in the Endless World, it changed from a reactive to a proactive state. From that act of Resistance were born the rules for revealing both light and Light.

THE LIGHT BULB METAPHOR APPLIED TO LIFE

★ The negative pole in a light bulb corresponds to our reactive desires.

★ The positive pole corresponds to all the fulfillment and Light we seek from life.

★ The filament corresponds to our free will to choose NOT to react, thus avoiding direct pleasure.

Just as the resistance of the filament keeps the light aglow in a bulb, resisting our reactive behavior keeps spiritual Light shining. When we fail to apply Resistance to our reactive impulses and we react, we create a short circuit. There is a direct connection occurring between our reactive desire (the negative pole) and the Light of pleasure (the positive pole). There is a momentary flash of self-indulgent delight followed by darkness, because the "bulb," the soul, has short-circuited and burned itself out.

A UNIVERSE OF RESISTANCE

The concept of revealing Light through Resistance is present in every area of our lives.

When we listen to a violinist play an instrument, the sound waves are created by the Resistance of the bow against the strings. We perceive the music when our eardrums resist the sound. That is the seemingly magical creative power of Resistance.

In a similar way, we've all seen those breathtaking images of the earth from space. Like a sparkling blue jewel, the earth radiates gloriously against the velvety blackness. Once again, the principle of Resistance is responsible. The earth's atmosphere resists the sun's light, creating illumination. But the void of space produces no Resistance whatsoever, and the result is darkness, though sunlight fills the vacuum.

Human beings possess free will to resist the pleasurable energy generated by reactive impulses. Free will can occur only if something terribly influential tries to persuade us not to resist—therein lies the purpose of the Satan and the obstacles he throws our way.

The Seventh Principle of Kabbalah states:

Resisting our reactive impulses creates lasting Light.

The Eight Principle of Kabbalah states:

Reactive behavior creates intense sparks of Light, but eventually leaves darkness in its wake.

SUPPRESSING VERSUS RESISTANCE

There is a very fine line and distinction between suppressing our emotions and shutting down our reactive systems. *Resistance* creates momentary struggle, but almost immediately there is calm and clarity. Suppressing emotions, on the other hand, creates long-term stress. Slowly, suppressed emotions gather force. Pressure builds and, eventually, we blow!

For example, if someone angers us and we truly apply the spiritual concept of Resistance toward our usual rash response, there is no animosity. No vengeance in our hearts. We do not feel insulted or hurt. If we feel any of those things, if we get caught up in the drama of the moment, it means we failed to recognize the spiritual opportunity of the situation. That's our clue.

When we recognize that anger and other negative emotions are just tests sent to us by the Light so we can remove Bread of Shame, we will know, with certainty, that we applied Resistance. We will feel the resplendent presence of the Light that has emerged from our spiritual action. We will *know*.

At first, the effort to resist will be a *combination* of suppression and authentic Resistance. That's okay. This effort will gradually remove layers of reactive emotions. Consistent efforts at Resistance will progressively cleanse reckless behavior, selfish desires, and negative thoughts. Certainty that we are drawing Light, and awareness of the process, are just as important as our attempts at Resistance. Resisting our reactive emotions is refined and perfected as we continue to undertake it. We become more proficient as we experience this process and internalize these spiritual principles.

COPING VERSUS RESISTANCE

When we resist the urge to react and create a space for the Light to enter our beings, this spiritual energy has a transforming effect on our consciousness. For instance, merely *coping* with an anxiety attack will not remove deep-seated fear or prevent an attack from recurring. Resistance, however, with the conviction that we are removing Bread of Shame, strikes at the seed of the problem; *knowing* with deep trust that we are transforming from *reactive* to *proactive* will cleanse and gradually remove the cause of the attack. In the dimension of the Light- in that other reality- negativity has no part. Through Resistance, we can enter that realm. And the connection remains with us forever.

THE JOY OF OBSTACLES: AN ALTERNATIVE VIEW OF LIFE'S CHALLENGES

As we've learned, spiritual transformation does not mean seeking refuge from the problems of life by lighting incense and chanting away our cares. Rather, we must confront our chaos and our reactions to it. To help us receive more spiritual Light into our lives, Kabbalah offers us the Ninth Principle which states:

Obstacles are our opportunity to connect to the Light.

The more barriers there are, the more chances we have to plug in to the Light. The more obstacles, the greater the number of triggers to ignite our reactions, so that we can resist and transform them. The more, the merrier! After all, *transforming* is the purpose of our lives (see Kabbalah's Fourth Principle) and only an obstacle can give us that opportunity!

WHEN BIGGER IS BETTER

The Resistance we apply in a situation also determines how much Light we receive. Imagine a tiny stone in space. It reflects and generates an amount of light relative to its size. Suppose we put a 50x50-foot sheet of mirror in space. More resistance is occurring; therefore, more Light is revealed.

This simple principle is the key to determining how much spiritual Light we generate. The more Light we push away or reflect, the more we receive. The more we resist our reactive behavior, the more happiness and pleasure radiate in our lives.

It works like this:

- **The bigger the problem, the stronger our urge to react.**

- **The bigger our reaction, the more Resistance we have to apply to stop it.**

- **The more Resistance we apply, the more spiritual Light in our lives.**

So remember the following Tenth Principle the

next time a formidable challenge looms on the horizon:

The greater the obstacle, the greater the potential Light.

THE PATH OF MOST RESISTANCE

Most people tend to choose the path of least Resistance in life. They look for the easy, comfortable situations. But staying comfortable doesn't generate lasting Light. We must learn to flee our comfort zones and plunge headfirst into uncomfortable situations. That is where we can apply the most Resistance. True, the path of most Resistance causes some pain and discomfort for a moment. But it's the only way to generate long-term fulfillment. Difficult though it may seem, we should embrace rather than avoid problems and obstacles. They are the true opportunities for spiritual development.

THE LAW OF "TIKUN"

In common with other spiritual traditions from around the world, Kabbalah teaches that each of us comes to this world with baggage from previous lifetimes. This baggage contains all the situations in which we short-circuited in our last lives or at some forgotten point in this life. Each time we fail to resist our reactive behavior, we have to correct it at some point in the future. This concept of correction is called "Tikun." We can have a *Tikun* with money, people, health, friendship, or relationships. There's an easy way to identify our personal *Tikun*. Whatever is uncomfortable for us is part of our *Tikun*!

All the people in our lives who truly bother and annoy us, they too are part of our *Tikun*. If we find it difficult to say no to a salesperson calling on the phone during dinner hour, that is our *Tikun* and it needs to be corrected. If we are embarrassed about asking for a discount from a haughty salesclerk in an upscale designer's shop, you can be sure that is our personal *Tikun* and area of correction. If we find it difficult to confront an employee or an employer, the root cause is found within the concept of *Tikun*.

When we fail to make a correction by resisting our reactive behavior, it becomes more difficult to correct next time around in that specific area. That particular reactive trait grows stronger. Our opponent grows stronger. Not only do we have to face the problem again, but it will be that much harder emotionally to activate Resistance. And next time around does not necessarily mean next life; these same corrections can appear over and over again in our present incarnations. Sometimes it's a little too easy to blame past-life behavior for the problems in this life. We usually do enough rotten stuff right here to warrant the chaos that afflicts us. This is the spiritual reason why the same problems keep recurring. They may very well manifest through different people or situations years later, but it's the same underlying problem again and again. Seeking comfort and avoiding our *Tikun* produces momentary gratification and relief, but it is linked to long-term chaos. In contrast, *the bigger the obstacle, the greater the potential Light*.

With this new understanding, we can no longer be victims. We can no longer lament the hardships, problems, and uncomfortable circumstances that confront us, no matter how good that might feel, because all those difficulties are there to call down the everlasting Light of fulfillment into our lives. But first, there is a *Tikun* situation demanding to be corrected.

GROUNDHOG DAY

If you haven't seen the film *Groundhog Day*, go out and rent the video the moment you close this book. It's a wonderful demonstration of the Kabbalistic principle of *Tikun* in action.

In the film, Bill Murray plays Phil Connors, a weatherman and the ultimate reactive character, consumed in his own self-indulgence, conceit, and indifference to the world around him. But Phil gets stuck in a time warp. He is trapped in the date of February 2 —Groundhog Day. The same day keeps repeating itself over and over again and no one knows this but him. It's fun at first, as Phil takes advantage of the situation, learning all he can about his world and the people in it in order to manipulate them and serve his own self-interests. But his world turns into a nightmare when the momentary pleasures wear off and not a drop of lasting fulfillment is to be found. Pushed to the point of suicide, he still awakes in the morning to find himself in the same town confronting the same events. There is no escape; not even death. Finally, after enduring tremendous suffering, he decides to change himself because he cannot change the world around him. He begins to perform good deeds and help the people who are experiencing the same misfortunes each day. Suddenly, he feels true fulfillment. Inspired by this Light, he goes on a rampage of sharing all over the town, winning the hearts of everyone. Eventually he winds up with the girl of his dreams, and the nightmare has ended. He has broken the recurring cycle and finds himself in a brand-new day, arm in arm with his true soul mate.

This is the law of *Tikun*, and this is the reason our lives sometimes feels like a bad movie that we're trapped in.

RESISTANCE AT WORK

Here are some situations to help enhance your understanding of Resistance and the opportunities that lie within difficult circumstances that are part of a *Tikun*:

RESISTING EGO

You're with a group of friends or business acquaintances. Everyone is talking, showing off their expertise about a particular topic, but it's obvious to you that you know much more than they do about the subject. You feel pressure to speak and flaunt your knowledge. Resist: It's your ego! Don't talk. Don't say a word. Recognize the spiritual opportunity and let it go. The Light will enter and you may learn something valuable from the conversation.

RESISTING INVERTED EGO

After a business presentation, everyone is asking questions except you. You feel pressured. Insecure. You're afraid of what the people in the room might be thinking about you. You become self-conscious. Your immediate reaction is to speak out of insecurity. This is inverted ego-thinking: *You are not good enough.* Resist! Let it go! Worrying about what others think is reactive behavior. Later, you'll probably have about a half dozen people approach you and strike up a conversation, making you feel really, really good about yourself.

RESISTING LAZINESS

A great idea comes to you. You are totally excited about it and are intent on acting upon it. Then procrastination sets in. You put it off. Resist this laziness! Resistance doesn't necessarily mean stopping and standing still. Often it means stopping the desire to stop and diving in head first. Your *Tikun* is not being able to finish what you start.

RESISTING JUDGMENT

An argument erupts between your family members or close friends. You hear one side of the story and are appalled. You're ready to pass judgment and choose sides. Resist! Let go of your emotions. Listen and hear the other side. Your *Tikun* is probably connected to judgmental behavior. You will discover that there are two sides to the story.

RESISTING SELF-INVOLVEMENT

You're confused over some important decisions, worried about their impact on your life. You self-deliberate, analyze, worry, fret, fuss, and stress out. Resist the urge to anguish over yourself! Go and do something good for someone else. Invest a little time helping others with their problems. When you get out of your own way, solutions will come to you when you least expect them.

RESISTING SELF-PRAISE

You did something really wonderful, and everyone admires you for it. You are now tempted to relive the glory and replay it over and over again in your mind. Resist these self-serving recollections! Think bigger. What else can you do? What's next? Move on to the next positive deed.

RESISTING EVIL IMPULSES

Things aren't going well. You're feeling a little down and a bit insecure about yourself. Suddenly, a friend calls. After a moment of small talk, the friend begins bad-mouthing another close friend. You get sucked into the conversation. Knocking down someone else makes you feel better about yourself. Hearing about someone else's problems makes you feel better about your own situation. Resist the desire to gossip and speak bad about others! Kabbalistically, the sin of murder is not limited to physical death; it includes character assassination. Terminating the conversation is therefore the equivalent of saving someone's life. This will reveal tremendous Light, which will truly help with your problems.

RESISTING CONTROL

You're a new writer who's just completed what you believe is a great manuscript. You show it to a friend who happens to be an editor. You're expecting high praise. But your friend criticizes it. You take the hard-hitting critique personally, and begin losing your confidence. Resist! Your reaction means you believe that you're the true source of this material, not the Light. True artists know they are just a channel. Moreover, even the criticism comes from the Light. So give up control. Trust the process and let go of your personal attachment to the work.

RESISTING GUILT

You did something wrong—really wrong—so you beat yourself up pretty badly. You lay the guilt on heavily. Resist the compulsion to self-destruct! Let it go. Embrace the Kabbalistic truth that there are two sides within each of us. Proactive and reactive. Light and darkness. The soul and the Satan. The part that needs correction and transformation, and the God-aspect of ourselves that will help us transform. Don't ignore the wrongdoing. But look at it as an opportunity. Falling spiritually and picking ourselves back up again is how we create spiritual transformation.

RESISTING EXPECTATIONS

You are full of expectations for your work, but they fail to materialize. You expect certain responses from friends; they let you down. You have clear ideas about the way certain people should treat you after all that you've done for them; they prove to be ungrateful. You have expectations about a long-awaited holiday; it rains every day and someone steals your credit cards. Resist all your feelings of disappointment! Stop those feelings of victimization. Something *better* is coming. Embrace the Kabbalistic principle of asking the Light for what you *need* in life, not for what you want. Later, you will see the real blessing and spiritual reason for the disappointment.

RESIST A LACK OF CONFIDENCE

You have to speak in public, or take responsibility for a major project. Your natural reaction might be, "I cannot do it, I'm not good enough, I don't want all the attention focused upon me." This is reversed ego. Let go of your limited thinking. It's not even about you. There's a bigger picture that includes other people, not just yourself.

RESISTING SELFISHNESS

You arrive home from a bustling day at work. An important business deal consumes your mind. Your children want your attention, but you are too preoccupied calculating all the facts and figures. You'll play with them another time—after all, you tell yourself, you are doing all this for your family. Rubbish! Resist those fanciful, self-serving reactions. It's really all about you. The thrill of the deal. The profit and power. These are common selfish desires. Give your kids your time when it's the most difficult. Even if you are having a hard time concentrating. They don't want another business deal. They want your love and attention. And don't get down on yourself and think you are a lousy father or husband when it's hard to focus during play. Resist that as well. The fact that you are conscious of what's happening, and making the effort, will bring Light to the situation. Recognize that the Satan is playing mind games with you. He's behind the whole thing—all your dreams of power and wealth. When the Satan is pulling your strings, no matter how high you climb, he will make you feel like it's never enough. In your relentless futile pursuit, your family will slip away. Resistance will prevent that from happening. Contrary to all those *Star Trek* flicks, Resistance is not futile. Resistance is fulfillment! The true Light that comes from family is often hard to reveal. The Satan can make the thrill of business feel better than the comforts of home—on the surface level, until it's too late. When, however, you apply the concept of Resistance, suddenly you will find a sense of contentment and joy you never knew before.

RESISTING INSECURITY

You and a partner worked long and hard on a project. It's a smashing success. Now you're afraid of giving away too much credit to your associate. You try to calculate who did what, out of your own insecurity. It will hurt your ego if everyone thinks your partner was the major contributor to the project. Resist those reactive thoughts and feelings! Then give away *all* the credit. Everything. Let go completely. As you are about to do this, you may think, I should only resist a little bit, not too much, because I have to practice all this Kabbalah stuff one step at a time. Balderdash! Resist these thoughts as well, and give all the credit to your partner. Remember, the Satan will test you every step of the way. Remember, praise gives pleasure for a moment; Light remains eternal. Don't trade away the farm for a bit of ego gratification.

RESISTING EMBARRASSMENT

You make a big mistake. If everyone notices, you'll turn purple and die of embarrassment. You react and try to cover it up. Resist! Love the humiliation. Take it all in. Lower your defenses. Lower your guard. Walk through the mishap slowly and soak up as much embarrassment as possible. Make yourself vulnerable. Recognize that this is an opportunity to wipe out your ego. In the end, your ego will be subjugated, and you will see that no one even noticed your error. That's how the Light works.

RESISTING EGO

You're out with friends and you're meeting new acquaintances. You're introduced by your friends as the smart one in your group. Now you feel pressure to respond to a difficult question, and you're not 100 percent sure of the answer. Your initial reaction is to fake it and ramble through as best as you can. Resist! Just say, "I don't know." Leave it at that. Then resist those reactive thoughts that tell you that your friends might not like, admire, or look up to you anymore.

RESISTING DOUBTS

You apply the wisdom of Kabbalah in your life. You use the principle of Resistance in a real-life situation. There are no results. Doubts flood your mind. *It doesn't work*, you say to yourself. Resist these reactive thoughts! It's a test to see if you've truly surrendered. Whenever you look for results, you've blown the entire exercise. That's the ultimate paradox. Look for results and they won't come. Give it up, and you'll get it all!

That's about all this book can do for you on this particular topic. The rest is up to you. You have to jump into the chaotic situations of life and "just do it." You will know the power and magic of Resistance when you experience it in real life.

But guess what? Once you've switched from reactive to proactive, you've removed Bread of Shame. You've spiritually transformed yourself in that situation. You are now ready and able to receive the everlasting Light of fulfillment in that part of your life. You have accomplished the purpose of your existence in that specific circumstance.

MILLION-DOLLAR CHALLENGE

Suppose you are in severe financial difficulty. God comes to you and says He will give you $1 million every time someone hurts you or angers you—provided you completely let go of any reactive feelings. Simply put, you cannot take anything personally.

What would be on your mind all day? You'd be praying for God to send you people to hurt you. You'd wake up every morning searching out all the difficult relationships and offensive people!

The fact is, when you live your life in that manner, you receive something more valuable than a million dollars. You receive the Light, which already includes financial sustenance, rejuvenation, well-being, happiness, and peace of mind.

We have been programmed to avoid problems and to despise obstacles. We have been conditioned to refute and rebut every opinion and argument put forth by our enemies and friends alike. The Satan plays a major role in creating this chaos, and the technique he uses is as old as humankind itself...

TEMPTATION

Recall a moment when a light bulb burst in your home. The bulb burst because the filament broke, allowing a direct connection between the positive and the negative poles. There was no Resistance occurring.

When a light bulb short-circuits and blows up, the momentary intensity of the flash is always far stronger than the light of the bulb under normal conditions. In the same way, momentary pleasure invoked by reactive behavior is much more powerful and intoxicating than the ongoing pleasure of Light that is generated by Resistance.

Our opponent flashes immense pleasure in front of our five senses at every opportunity. All too often we accept his offer, because reactive behavior is very tempting. It delivers an overwhelming burst of energy.

The intensity of resisted Light may not be as brilliant as the flash of a short circuit, but the volume of illumination produced by Resistance is far greater.

Drugs and alcohol similarly demonstrate the power of a short circuit. According to Kabbalah, intoxicants do elevate the soul to higher levels of the spiritual atmosphere. As psychoanalyst Carl Jung pointed out, it is not by accident that alcohol is also called spirits. The problem is, drugs connect us very directly to these energy forces. As a result, we short-circuit. We crash. We burn, and then we burn out.

Kabbalist Rav Berg makes an important distinction between moralistic reasons for abstaining from drugs versus the Kabbalistic viewpoint. While it is our purpose in life to ascend to higher states of consciousness, drugs and alcohol are completely inadequate to fulfill this intention. We need to find ways of achieving that higher state of existence *permanently* rather than momentarily. But the Satan constantly uses the power of instant gratification and momentary highs and "rushes" to ignite our reactions. His sole purpose is to create short circuits, directly, so that we will eventually plunge ourselves into darkness.

CRASH DIET

Barbara is 30 pounds overweight. She has been dieting and exercising for a couple of weeks. But then someone kindly offers her a piece of chocolate cake, her favorite. The reactive instinct of her body is to thankfully accept. But a conflict brews in Barbara's mind: Should she give up the diet for now and start again on Monday, or stick with the program?

Barbara attempts to arouse her willpower. She summons as much strength as she can while she tries to remember the passion behind her initial pledge to lose weight. She desperately wants to find that original sense of dedication toward a healthier lifestyle. Yes, she wants to fit into her old jeans again! Barbara wants to hold true to her goal of losing the weight. She knows she must resist.

Suddenly, someone else is on the scene. The Satan fills Barbara's mind with desires that are richly vivid and compelling, and Barbara is slowly breaking down at the thought of licking creamy fudge off a fork. She finally succumbs to the reactive urge.

Once she has surrendered control, she might as

well eat the cake for all it's worth. At least, that's what the opponent tells her. And she does eat it. And it tastes wonderful. Soon Barbara's body is enjoying a sugar rush. And the cannabinoids in the chocolate are inducing the same kind of high that marijuana delivers. And the chocolate acts as a cheap substitute for love because it contains a stimulating substance that generates the rush we feel when we fall in love. The cocoa fat is prompting the production of opiates in Barbara's brain, which arouse further feelings of pleasure. And then there is that old favorite, caffeine, which is stimulating her brain and pumping adrenaline through her veins. Instant gratification!

But the story is not over yet. Suddenly, the rush of pleasure wears off. Barbara's blood sugar plummets. She crashes. Kabbalistically, the Light from the cake has been cut off in a short circuit. Barbara is now overwhelmed by all-too-familiar feelings of guilt, regret, depression, and disappointment.

If Barbara had resisted her reactive desire to consume the cake and had eaten an apple instead, her body and soul would have felt satiated. Not in an intense way, but in a tempered, balanced, and fulfilling way. More important, 24 hours later, feelings of accomplishment, self-worth, and fulfillment would have remained with her.

We face tough decisions every day, in business, social situations, and family life. Do we continue reacting to all the external stimuli coming from every direction? Or do we stop the reactions in order to bring a bit of spiritual sanity into our lives?

For some reason, it's just not easy to resist immediate gratification. We set our minds toward the goal of not reacting, but when the time comes, we're ambushed by the fleeting pleasures of a reactive moment. As we read these ideas in this book, we get excited for the moment. Next day, someone insults us, a business deal falls through, someone speaks badly of us, and we fall back into our reactive ways.

Before we discover why we have such difficulty resisting temptation, we must reveal another weapon in the Satan's arsenal.

THE FAUSTIAN PACT

Whenever things start going really well, we may fall into the trap of believing that good times will never end. We become arrogant. We believe we are infallible.

Kabbalah teaches us that Light comes from two sources—the Creator and the Satan. Remember, the Light of the Creator is an eternal flame. The Light of the Satan is the bright flash from a stick of dynamite. When we strive for success with reactive behavior, our success comes from the Satan. The more reactive we are, the more success we generate—at a price!

According to Kabbalah, the Faustian myth of selling one's soul to the Devil is very close to the truth. The Faustian principle is at work almost every day: Be reactive and the Satan will give you Light, albeit temporarily. When that Light is taken away, the Satan gets to keep the real Light of the Creator. You get to keep the chaos after the dynamite blows.

Kabbalah teaches us that the Satan will pay us well for a while just to keep us in a reactive state of mind. In other words, he simply gives us a stick of dynamite with an extra-long fuse (time) so that the illusion of success and Light lasts longer. When we are flying high, we believe that we are the brilliant orchestrators of our own success. Our egos are inflated to the size of the Goodyear blimp, and just as full of hot air. And when we least expect it, it deflates.

SLAVERY

Most everyone is familiar with the Biblical story of the Exodus. But most people, including most rabbis and priests, don't recognize the hidden spiritual significance of this story and its clear importance in our own lives:

The story tells us that the Israelites were in bondage in Egypt for 400 years. They were slaves and the children of slaves, held captive to the hardhearted Pharaoh, ruler of Egypt. There came a great leader by the name of Moses, who, on a mission from God, won the freedom of his people. Moses then led the former slaves on a long and arduous journey, which included that famous detour through the Red Sea, and on to Mount Sinai for a date with destiny.

But here's the interesting part. The Israelites were tasting freedom for the first time in centuries, yet they still managed to complain, whine, and grumble the moment it got a little hot and sticky in the desert. They actually begged Moses to take them back to Egypt!

Rabbi Isaac Luria, the eminent renaissance Kabbalist, revealed that this entire story is a code.

Egypt is a code word for the human ego and humanity's incessantly reactive nature. This is truly the oldest master-slave relationship in Creation.

All of us are held in bondage by our reactive urges. Our egos, and the Satan who controls them, are our true taskmasters—and he is so good at his job, most of us don't even realize we are in bondage.

We are enslaved to the physical world around us. We are held captive to our careers, relationships, fears, and anxieties. We are incarcerated by our own desperate need for other people's acceptance. Any aspect of our natures that controls us is *Egypt*.

But through awareness that we are still imprisoned in Egypt, we can grasp the key that unlocks the chains.

This is the true spiritual power of Kabbalah. It is the power to gain freedom from ourselves.

THE POWER OF CERTAINTY

Fleeing the Egyptians, the Israelites were cornered on the banks of the Red Sea. Pharaoh and his army raced toward them, bent on their total annihilation. Suddenly the Red Sea parted, producing two massive walls of water that reached to the sky. According to the Zohar, all the waters of the earth split and rose toward the heavens. And the Israelites raced off to freedom.

When Pharaoh and his army were approaching, Moses had cried out to God for help. The Zohar teaches that God replied with a mysterious question: "Why are you calling to me?" Concealed within this question is a profound spiritual truth. God did not part the Red Sea! In fact, God was surprised that Moses even called upon Him at that moment. But if the almighty Creator did not part the waters, who did?

Many thousands of years later, another crisis took place. It was not a life-or-death situation, but it definitely seemed like one at the time. Although the names have been changed, this story is true.

Michael owned a direct-sales organization with offices across North America. After one of the best fourth-quarter sales periods in his company's history,

Michael headed off to Miami with his wife and children for a ten-day holiday.

On his first day back, Michael's accountant walked into his office. With obvious discomfort, the accountant explained that one of the company's sales managers had sent in phony deposit slips for his sales during the last three weeks of December. The money had never made it into the company's bank account. Worse, this was their best manager, with the best performing office in the organization.

"How much is missing?" Michael asked.

His accountant swallowed hard and told him, "The manager stole $105,000."

Michael poured himself a glass of water and took a small sip. As Michael remembers it: "At that moment I had a serious choice to make, and I had to make it fast. I could practice what I learned in my Kabbalah classes, or I throw it all out the window because of the large amount of money that was at stake. It was up to me..."

A great deal of time had passed between the parting of the Red Sea and Michael's loss of more than $100,000. But it was knowledge of Kabbalah that enabled both the ancient Israelites and a contemporary suburbanite to discover startling solutions to their predicaments.

THE CERTAINTY PRINCIPLE

At that moment, Michael had a decision to make. Should he *react* with fear, panic, and anger? Or should he call upon what he'd learned in his studies of Kabbalah—including the hidden lesson of the Red Sea's parting—and choose a *proactive* alternative?

Here's what Michael had learned regarding the dire straits of the Israelites as they stood on the brink of destruction.

We know that the Israelites did escape. And, yes, the Red Sea (and *all* the waters of the earth) did part magnificently. *But God didn't do it.*

When God asked Moses why he was calling upon Him, God was implying that Moses and the Israelites had the power to part the Red Sea on their own. God was revealing one of the Spiritual Laws of Life: Overcome your own reactive nature and the heavens will respond and help you overcome the laws of Mother Nature, for the two are intimately connected. Doing that requires total *certainty*.

That is the secret interpretation of this story.

The Israelites were forced to step into the waters of the sea and proceed with *total certainty* before a drop of water began to split. They were required to resist the overwhelming uncertainty that was ingrained into their natures.

In fact, Kabbalistic sages explained that the Red Sea did not part until the waters had reached the nostrils of the Israelites. And then, when the waters rushed into their throats, the Israelites relinquished control and demonstrated certainty in a positive outcome. They put their lives into the hands of the Light. A split second later, they were breathing fresh air as the waters parted and rose toward the heavens.

Michael was also on the verge of drowning. He looked at his accountant and said, "The manager never stole the money. The money is not missing."

Then he added, "You can never lose something that is really yours. Therefore, the money has to show up. If it doesn't, it was never mine to begin with."

Michael was injecting proactivity into the situation. He would not react to *either* outcome. He was certain that, whatever the outcome, it would be best for his spiritual understanding and growth.

His accountant was also certain—he was sure that Michael had gone off the deep end!

"Do I just stand here and do nothing?" the accountant cried. "Shouldn't we call the police and start an investigation? We are trying to run a company here!"

The accountant was completely locked into his belief that the money had been stolen. It took Michael an hour to convince him to be even slightly open to another possibility.

"First," Michael said, "I want you to accept the possibility that the money is not missing. Second, if it is missing, it was never ours. We would have lost it in another deal, or our profits would be lower next year by the same amount because our sales would fall. In other words, have the certainty that whatever happens, it is correct. We must have certainty that the outcome will be the best from a spiritual perspective. Once you have that state of mind, then continue on and do what you would normally do in this situation."

Although the accountant did not fully understand what Michael was talking about, he did come back the next morning with the news that $88,000 had suddenly turned up in a bank in Winnipeg, Manitoba, Canada.

"We found the checks," the accountant explained. The manager could not cash them so he deposited the checks and kept all the cash.

"No," Michael replied, "the manager did not steal the cash. The cash will also turn up. No one can take what is rightfully ours. And if it doesn't show up, it was not ours to begin with."

Michael was again making a proactive attempt not to be a slave, or to be under the control of any outcome, positive or negative. As it turned out, the manager had indeed intended to steal the money. But by the time he reached Florida, a couple of days later, he had a change of heart. He actually called Michael on the phone and confessed.

"There's no doubt in my mind my that the Kabbalistic concept of certainty played a major role in what happened," Michael said later. "Before I learned Kabbalah, I would have sent two guys with baseball bats to hunt the thief down. They probably would have never found him, and I'd still be out over

$100,000. My blood pressure would have skyrocketed throughout this whole sordid affair and I'd be living a life filled with feelings of revenge, victimization, and negativity. Thankfully, I'm free of all that."

According to many spiritual teachings, Kabbalah included, consciousness creates our reality. What we desire is what we receive. If we are uncertain, we receive the energy of uncertainty. If we respond to crises with worry and negative thinking, we increase the likelihood of a painful outcome.

But it could all be very different. We can put an end to our uncertainty and doubt. We can disrupt the Satan's agenda. By offering Resistance, we create a space for the Light to fill.

If you want to see real miracles occur, try shutting down thoughts of uncertainty about positive outcomes. Start focusing on removing Bread of Shame and shift your focus away from results and outcomes. Remember, we already had the results in the Endless World. Michael already had the joy that comes from $100,000 cash in your pocket. What Michael did not have in the Endless World was the ability to be proactive. He gained this opportunity in this world when the money departed and he did not react. Once Michael seized this opportunity to remove Bread of Shame and transform from reactive to proactive, he accomplished the original objective of the Vessel—to become the cause of his own fulfillment as opposed to being a reactive effect; to create something new—a proactive consciousness instead of reactive one. Once this feat was accomplished, the Light was allowed to flow freely. The money was free to return because the purpose of creation was achieved. If Michael had reacted, he would have missed the opportunity and the money would have vanished for good. Worse, he would have been forced to confront a similar challenge (opportunity) again at some point in the future, because there was still a *Tikun*, a transformation waiting to take place.

To help maintain a proactive state of mind in difficult situations, we have the Eleventh Kabbalistic Principle:

> *When challenges appear overwhelming, inject certainty. The Light is always there!*

Injecting certainty into a situation does not mean we always get the result we want. Rather, certainty means knowing the Light's unseen hand is in the game with us. There may be times when we are behind on the scoreboard, but ultimately we can't lose.

Kabbalah teaches that the *adversity* in any situation is the truly positive element. Just as the antidote to a poisonous snakebite is contained in the venom, the Light is contained within the obstacles of life.

When we understand this principle, we enthusiastically embrace life's difficulties. We recognize them as opportunities to remove Bread of Shame and to become true Creators in our lives.

Remember, certainty does not mean we get what we want, but rather we get what we need in our lives to further our spiritual growth. It's having certainty in whatever outcome is placed before us. It's accepting responsibility for the negativity that strikes in our lives. It's recognizing that the rotten stuff that is in our face because we've planted a negative seed at some point in our past. When we overcome our uncertainty, we create miracles in our lives.

THE POWER OF PERMANENT CHANGE

One day, a striking brunette woman visits her favorite salon and dyes her hair blond. The sudden shift in hair color, however, is only a superficial change because her true hair color is determined by the DNA in her genes. All the hair coloring and tinting in the world is not going to change the fact that she's a brunette. Consequently, a few weeks later, dark roots begin to reemerge on her head.

How many times have we attempted to initiate change in our behavior and lifestyle but ended up reverting back to our old ways? How many of us have the emotional and spiritual strength to permanently stop our inborn reactions dead in their tracks? How many of us have the natural foresight to always see beyond the immediate moment and not get upset or panic when a nasty problem arises?

According to Kabbalah, no one individual has such power. And that is why lasting change and peace have failed to take hold. So the ancient sages provided us with the tools of Kabbalah, which strike at the root level of our existence.

PART FIVE

DNA OF THE SOUL

THE ALPHABET OF CREATION

Among the Blessed One's kindness to His creations is having prepared for them the way to rise from the pit of their deeds and to escape the trap of their offenses; to save themselves from destruction and to turn away His wrath from them.

— *The Gates of Repentance*

Everyone has heard of the human genetic code known by the initials DNA, but few people outside the scientific community can say what DNA is or describe what it really does. DNA is best described as an instruction manual for our cells. All cells begin in an undifferentiated state. Our DNA then determines which cells will evolve to become internal organs, bone, brain matter, or other tissues. Today, science is turning to gene therapy for cures to many serious diseases, because if we can change the DNA instructions, we can change the human being.

Like all instruction manuals, DNA is written in a language utilizing an alphabet. In the late 1950s, geneticists cracked the genetic code of life and determined that the DNA alphabet is composed of four "letters," which they designated as A, T, C, and G.

A, T, C, and G refer to four different kinds of nucleotides. These four nucleotides combine to create 20 amino acids, which produce the "words" and "sentences" composing the genetic code of every individual. Human beings have about 3 billion letters in our genetic codes. The differences between individuals lie in the combination and sequences of our four nucleotides. A complete copy of our DNA instruction manual is contained inside each cell of our bodies. Each cell contains the whole 3-billion-letter library.

All we really are, in a physical sense, is a set of living letters. A living, walking, breathing, talking alphabet.

What's more, the entire universe is alphabetic in nature. Just as letters combine to form words, atoms combine to create more complicated structures such as molecules. Just as words combine to form sentences, molecules combine to create various kinds of matter.

The renowned astrophysicist Hubert Reeves

gives examples of our alphabetic universe in his book, *The Hour of Our Delight*. Reeves writes:

> *In chemistry, water is a word composed of two letters, called hydrogen and oxygen.... The immense variety of gems, minerals, and rock formations derives from the combination of only a small number of atoms: oxygen, silicon, iron, calcium, aluminum, magnesium, and a few others. With these letters we can write the whole of geology.... As we explore our solar system, the stars in our Milky Way and those in more exotic galaxies, we find that the same atoms occur everywhere and combine according to the same laws. This atomic language is resolutely universal.*

Reeves concludes that nature is not structured like a language, but on the contrary, language is structured like nature.

Remarkably, all this information about DNA and the alphabetically structured universe was discovered recently, during the last 50 years. Even more remarkable was a man who lived some 4,000 years ago—a man who might best be described as the world's first geneticist. His name was Abraham, and he is the father of Judaism, Christianity, and Islam.

Abraham was the author of the very first known book on Kabbalah, *The Book of Formation*. This ancient Kabbalistic manuscript predates the Bible by many centuries. In *The Book of Formation*, Abraham wrote that the entire universe had its own genetic-like building blocks. Moreover, he said these building blocks were alphabetic in nature. Abraham described a series of primal energy forces, like cosmic nucleotides, that combined to form all spiritual and physical reality.

More specifically, Abraham revealed how the unified Light of the Creator fragmented into 22 distinct forces to create our universe.

This is a wonderful, mystical notion. Perhaps even more wonderfully, we too can become poets of creation, using the Creator's alphabet to inscribe a new book of our lives. We can become spiritual geneticists, using the 22 letters to reengineer our souls' genetic makeup. We can alter our reactive natures and transform our lives.

But what are these 22 primordial forces? How do we harness and control them?

THE 22 FORCES OF CREATION

Twenty-two foundation letters: He engraved them, He carved them, He permuted them, He weighed them, He transformed them, and with them He depicted all that was formed and all that would be formed.

— *Abraham, The Book of Formation*

Abraham wrote that the 22 energy forces manifest in our world as 22 frequency patterns. They appear as shapes and vibrations that we can both visualize and vocalize. The 22 shapes are shown below. *They are the letters of the Hebrew alphabet.* Scan them from right to left.

א ב ג ד ה ו ז ח ט י כ ל מ נ ס ע פ צ ק ר ש ת

Kabbalah teaches that these letters were present at the very moment of Creation, not as letters written on a piece of parchment, but as magnificent forces of primordial energy. The Hebrew letters are instruments of power. In fact, the Hebrew word for "letter" actually means *pulse* or *vibration*, indicating a flow of energy. By virtue of its shape, sound, and vibration, a letter acts as an antenna that arouses and harnesses the energy of the universe.

232

UNIVERSAL ALPHABET

The letters of the Hebrew alphabet transcend religion, race, geography, and the very concept of language. Their influence is universal. Their scope, sweeping. Their power is shared with *all* humankind, though this controversial truth has been buried away for millennia.

Some of the greatest thinkers in history understood their universal truth and might. Scientists. Philosophers. Mathematicians. Physicians.

Consider the great Renaissance philosopher and physician Francis Mercury van Helmont (1614–1698). According to scholar Allison Coudert, van Helmont helped shape the evolvement of contemporary science. He consorted with the likes of Sir Isaac Newton and had a profound effect on Gottfried Wilhelm Leibniz, who invented calculus in 1684 and is considered to be one of the supreme intellects of the 17th century.

Francis Mercury van Helmont studied Kabbalah. He was a hip intellectual and a kind soul that graced his generation. Van Helmont and his peers were convinced that Hebrew was the universal alphabet of the cosmos and that *all* mankind could benefit from its power. He called it the "Natural Alphabet" and wrote a book titled the same. Coming from a Catholic-born physician, this was a bold perspective. In her book, *The Impact of the Kabbalah in the 17th Century: The Life and Thought of Francis Mercury van Helmont (1614–1698)*, Allison Coudert states that van Helmont believed that the mystical powers of Hebrew letters could ultimately:

"...reveal answers to every single question exercising the human mind about God and the universe."

Coudert writes that another Renaissance scholar, Johannes Reuchlin, concurred with van Helmont:

Reuchlin believed that Kabbalah was the "well" from which all later cultures and philosophies drew their ideas.

Hebrew was the uncorrupted and divine language of creation. "The speech of the Hebrews is simple, pure, uncorrupted, holy, brief, and constant." It is the language of God's revelation to man. The study of Hebrew grammar is therefore important as the key to unlock these divine secrets.

HEBREWTEK

Modern-day physicians also concur with the ancient physician van Helmont.

Consider the case of Dr. Artur Spokojny. Spokojny is a board-certified internist and cardiologist. He studied medicine at Harvard and graduated *summa cum laude* at Düsseldorf University. Spokojny, who was instrumental in developing laser treatments for heart disease, holds a faculty position at Cornell Medical College and maintains privileges at New York Presbyterian Hospital. Since 1988, he has been assistant director of the Catheterization Center at New York Hospital. Dr. Spokojny tells this story about one of his own patients:

"A patient was rushed into the ER with a heart attack. He was conscious, but I was worried because his heart rate was terribly slow. I asked that he be taken to the lab, and his heart actually stopped twice on the way. As it turned out, his right coronary artery was completely blocked. We worked on him for about 30 minutes, but nothing was helping. Whatever we tried failed. I felt so helpless. My last option was to start meditating intensely

235

upon a sequence of Hebrew letters מהש׳ *used for healing."*

"I could feel something happening while I was visualizing them. Out of nowhere, the blocked artery opened! What was unexplainable was the massive blood clot in the artery. It should have prevented the artery from opening. "

"When the whole ordeal was over, there was absolutely no damage to the heart. Nothing. No evidence of a heart attack. "

"The patient told me that during this episode he dreamed he was trapped inside a computer monitor. All the doors were locked shut. Suddenly, he found the right sequence of letters for the password. It opened the doors and he escaped. The other doctors had no idea what happened. We discussed it but couldn't come up with an explanation. I was unwilling to tell them what I had done, so the mystery remained unsolved."

PRACTICAL BENEFITS

Varied sequences of letters release enormous amounts of spiritual influences that give us the emotional power and inner strength to stop our reactive behavior. Different combinations of letters create different blends of energy, just as different combinations of musical notes create different melodies. The Light they emit purifies our hearts. Their spiritual influences cleanse destructive impulses from our being. Their sacred energy removes rash intolerant emotions, fear and anxiety. They have the power to help us transform from being hot-tempered tyrants into balanced compassionate beings. The letters can arouse healing, financial sustenance, and emotional well-being.

THE EYES ARE THE WINDOWS TO THE SOUL

Many of us might not have the ability to read Hebrew. Does this hindrance render the power of the letters ineffective? Not in the least. In fact, the ancient sages teach us that the eyes are the windows to the soul. The soul recognizes the forces of Creation as expressed through the Hebrew letters. One of the most powerful ways for those not versed in the pronunciation of the Hebrew letters to capture their energy is through simple visual contact. Like scanning.

THE POWER OF SCANNING

We are all familiar with the bar codes on items in a retail store. When flashed across the scanner, they provide an infinite amount of information, which the scanner processes in seconds. The scanner eliminates pricing errors, tracks inventory instantaneously, and saves time, effort, and money. If an inanimate object such as a bar-code scanner can produce such activity, imagine what the human mind can do.

Meditating, or just visually scanning these letters and their various sequences helps to arouse an abundance of spiritual forces. Consider it a "visual incantation." Or an "optical mantra." Interacting with these letters, in any way possible, gives us a direct but subconscious connection to our souls and the 99 percent realm of reality. Just as the shape of a key is the mechanism by which we open a door, the specific shapes of the Hebrew letters are the keys to open the doorway to the soul.

Science has recognized that human beings make use of only 10 percent of our full potential consciousness. But when we scan, meditate, and visually interact with the letters, we access the remaining major segment of our consciousness. Our subconscious absorbs the power and spiritual influences emanating from each word.

RESONANCE

When the eye scans the shapes of the Hebrew letters, a resonance is created between the Light and our souls. The same principle can be seen in a pair of tuning forks. When one fork is tapped, a resonance is created in the other, and the sound is duplicated. The human soul and the forces contained within the Hebrew letters are both formed from the blazing Light of the Creator. When the two are in proximity—achieved by visually scanning, meditating, or reciting the letters—a resonance is created and the energy of the letters is duplicated in the soul.

And here you have the Twelfth Principle of Spirituality:

True internal change is created through the DNA power of the Hebrew letters.

THE LIGHT OF THE LETTERS IN ACTION

Unique sequences of letters act as a conditioning agent that weakens and washes away our reactive impulses from our nature. The letters infuse us with inner strength and discipline to apply Resistance and cease our reactive moments. They target our opponent—our ego—in all its various manifestations. The moment we stop our reactive behavior, we are proactive and God-like. And then positive change begins. Dramatic shifts take place concerning our destinies and our fortunes in life as the Light of the 99 percent illumines that aspect of our existence.

Each small proactive step gives us lasting fulfillment in that one specific area of life where we effected a transformation. The number of areas to be addressed is large, however. We are faced with steps in business and in our relationships as parents, as spouses, and as friends. We must transform our reactive natures in each area of our lives. To accomplish that, we have been given a set of tools that are as old as time itself. It starts with the *72 Names of God*.

THE 72 NAMES OF GOD

When Moses parted the Red Sea, he used a very powerful spiritual technology combined with the power of certainty. He had possession of a formula that literally gave him access to the subatomic realm of nature.

The formula Moses used to overcome the laws of nature was hidden in the *Zohar*. For 2,000 years, only a few righteous people were aware of this formula. Now, with the sudden renaissance of Kabbalah, the formula has finally been revealed to the world.

This is the formula:

כהת	אכא	כלה	מהש	עלם	סיט	ילי	והו
הקם	הרי	מבה	יזל	ההע	לאו	אלד	הזי
וזו	מלה	ייי	נלך	פהל	כוו	כלי	לאו
ושר	לכב	אום	ריי	שאה	ירת	האא	נתה
ייז	רהע	וזעם	אני	מנד	כוק	כהת	יוז
מיה	עשל	ערי	סאל	ילה	וול	מיכ	ההה
פוי	מבה	נית	ננא	עמם	הוע	רני	והו
מוזי	ענו	יהה	ומב	מצר	הרח	ייל	נמם
מום	היי	יבמ	ראה	וזבו	איע	מנק	דמב

This formula is called the 72 Names of God. These are not names like Betty, Bill, and Barbara, but 72 sequences that have extraordinary power to overcome the laws of nature in all forms, including human nature. These three-letter sequences are the conduits that transmit various energies of the Light into our physical world. The power of these letters has been documented in the modern world. Dr. Spokojny tells another story concerning one of his patients:

"A male patient was having an operation on his aortic aneurysm. After surgery, his heart became arrhythmic and kept stopping. I was going to do a catheterization but I literally couldn't get him off the table without his heart stopping. I called in more specialists. We gave him all kinds of medication to stabilize him. Nothing worked. His heart kept stopping. We had to countershock him repeatedly to restart his heart. I knew we were going to lose him. "

"I went into my office and began scanning the Zohar, volume 15, which the Kabbalists say has tremendous healing power. After a few minutes of meditation, I came out of the office and he was

stable. The man literally walked out of the hospital without any damage to his heart. "

"How do I explain it? I can't. "

"But I will say this: In my opinion, the human body is like a computer. Like any computer, it requires an operating system to function properly. When a computer becomes corrupted, you have to reinstall the operating system. Sometimes you use antivirus software to debug the system. The same principle is at work here. Scanning or meditating on the Hebrew letters is like downloading and installing a new operating system in the body. Other sequences of letters work like an antivirus software that debug the immune system of the body."

Ten of the 72 Names are presented here, together with the purposes for which they can be used. Though you probably don't know Hebrew, you can still scan or meditate on the characters. Simply look with focused attention at each character, always remembering to scan from right to left. (Incidentally, these sequences are not words, nor are they pronounceable in any way that matters here.)

TO REMOVE COMPULSIVE OR
RECURRING NEGATIVE THOUGHTS

Everyone, to one degree or another, displays a form of obsessive behavior. Obsessive behavior can be quite distressing as it impels us to perform repetitive rituals that interfere with daily living. Some of us:

Dress ourselves in a specific order…

Walk a certain way…

Drive a particular route…

Continually clean and tidy our homes…

Check locks, lights, and switches…

Count things in a distinctive way…

We believe this ritualistic behavior will prevent some catastrophic event from taking place.

Obsessive behavior begins with compulsive thoughts. These intrusive thoughts torment our consciousness until we either perform the ritual or become ridden with anxiety. These recurrent unwanted thoughts can include *constant doubt, uncertainty, incessant worrying, dread, and excessive fear.* According to medical science, the neurotransmitter serotonin appears to play a key role in this disorder. However, Kabbalah asks, Why is serotonin causing a problem in the first place? All physical ailments have a spiritual cause, and we must travel to the root level in order to effect genuine change.

These spiritual forces help switch off destructive and oppressive thoughts by attacking the problem at the seed level—the soul and consciousness of the individual. By helping us shut down our negative mental processes, the spiritual forces free our minds of these obsessive thoughts and automatically curb negative behavior.

TO AROUSE TOTAL CERTAINTY
IN ANY SITUATION

There is only one way to render all the tools and principles of Kabbalah inoperative and worthless. It is called uncertainty. If we are doubtful or uncertain about any aspect of Kabbalistic teachings, we literally pull the plug and shut them down. "I'll believe it when I see it," must be replaced by, "When I believe it, then I'll see it!" In life, certainty is not about receiving what we want, but rather, certainty means recognizing that we are receiving what we need for spiritual growth.

When we face situations that ignite our doubts and uncertainties, these letters will awaken certainty, conviction, and trust.

TO AROUSE HEALING POWER

This sequence is composed of the same letters that spell out the name *Moses*, but are in a different order. Moses was a spiritual leader to the nation he helped forge in the Sinai desert. The Kabbalists tell us that the DNA-like letters that compose his name hold great spiritual power.

When Moses' Hebrew name is rearranged into this pattern, the letters transmit powerful healing forces—but to fully activate this power, we must think of others who are in need of healing. As this energy passes through us to assist other people, we automatically receive the benefits ourselves. It's best to visualize blue or white light radiating through the letters, and use this light to bathe the entire body or a specific area in need of healing.

TO REMOVE NEGATIVE FORCES FROM PEOPLE OR PLACES

Kabbalah teaches that contact with negative places and unpleasant people can influence our lives. Each of us has a spiritual field of energy that extends 88 inches from our bodies, according to Kabbalistic sages. If this field is charged with negative energy, it can lower our state of being causing sadness, depression, hostility, or doubts.

If you are confronted with a potentially destructive situation or person, visualizing these letters will help you nullify any negative force.

TO GENERATE THE ENERGY OF FINANCIAL SUSTENANCE

If you believe that you are the architect of your own success, you are reacting to your ego and doubting the existence of the Light. If fortunes are continually won and lost in your life, if you find yourself continually on a financial roller-coaster, if your wealth has been accumulated at the expense of relationships or good health, it is because you have been drawing wealth through the reactive system of human nature, leaving the opponent in complete control of your finances and life.

You must realize that all good fortune originates from the Light of the Creator. Meditating upon this sequence is an acknowledgment of this spiritual truth. These letters ensure that you draw your good fortune from the Light and not from the opponent.

TO REMOVE EGOMANIA

Most of us are under the delusion that we act freely. In truth, we are enslaved to our egos and to ego-based aspects of our material existence. We are held captive to our jobs, our mortgages, our clothes, or our need to outdo others.

This sequence helps unlock and remove the shackles of ego, offering us the greatest freedom a person can attain—freedom from the self. These spiritual influences impress within us the wisdom and strength to resist trading away life's true pleasures—marriage, children, friendship, and spiritual fulfillment—for the fleeting pleasures generated by gratifying our own egos.

TO REMOVE THE FORCE OF DEATH

The experience of death is not limited to just the physical body. Death manifests itself in the end of relationships, the failure of a business, the demise of a marriage, or the loss of happiness.

By confronting death at the most basic level, we can avert many of the "fatalities" that occur in all areas of life. This formation of letters helps eliminate the destructive influence of the Angel of Death. When scanning, visualize any area of endeavor that is in danger of coming to an end.

TO RETURN TO THE SEED LEVEL OF OUR EXISTENCE

A principle of physics states that for every action there is an equal and opposite reaction. For every cause there is an effect. In our physical world, there is a gap between cause and effect. As we've learned, Kabbalah defines this divide as *time*.

- Time is the measurement between conduct and retribution.

- Time is the span between behavior and repercussion.

- Time is the chasm between crime and consequence.

Because of time's existence, we believe, mistakenly, that goodness goes unrewarded; that evil goes unpunished; that life lacks true justice. Moreover, we tend to forget the negative deeds that we, ourselves, committed as time passes. Negative behavior encompasses more than just murder. A few unkind words to our neighbor, spouse, or friend sets the cause-and-effect principle into motion as well. In fact, sometimes assassinating a person's characters or destroying their self-esteem is just as negative as committing physical homicide.

The Light emitted through this sequence of letters returns us to the causal level of our existence. Consider this the ultimate "time-tunnel" effect. We have an opportunity to positively alter the negative seeds that we planted long ago. Thoughtful meditation coupled with penitence in our hearts for prior misdeeds helps us alter our past, reshape the present, and secure a more fulfilling future.

THE STRENGTH TO STAND AFTER WE FALL

Climbing the path of spirituality is perhaps the most difficult challenge we face. The *Zohar* says a person requires far more greatness and strength to ascend the spiritual ladder than to conquer nations or amass great wealth in the material world. Accordingly, the Kabbalistic path is fraught with obstacles and tests. Sometimes these tests knock us off our feet. When we lose our spiritual balance, it's important to stand up again rather than sink into doubt and depression. Our opponent utilizes a twofold plan of attack.

1. Make us fall.

2. Keep us down through feelings of guilt and disappointment over our fall.

Getting back up again generally generates greater spiritual Light in the world than if we had never fallen in the first place. Thus, the fact that we fell is not what's important. The act of rising up again is where true greatness is found. This sacred Name of God imbues us with the emotional strength to stand after we stumble; to rise after we fall; to endure when the path seems unendurable.

THE COURAGE TO SPEAK
AND HEAR THE TRUTH

There are moments when it becomes difficult for us to be lovingly truthful with others. Emotional blocks and fears can tower over us just like the highest mountain. Our hearts race, our adrenaline pumps at the prospect of speaking our minds. It's easier to tell people what they want to hear. Then again, it can be equally frightful to confront painful truths about ourselves—forcing our friends to tell us only what we want to hear.

Here we receive the spiritual strength and courage to make those external and internal confrontations. The letters summon the resolve to speak those difficult words of truth to our friends. And because these truths can often hurt, the Light awakens compassion so that our words are born of love, not anger. Courage is invoked so that we're open to hear which of our traits taint our own hearts, which of our imperfect qualities cause pain to others.

ACCOUNTABILITY

There is an old teaching given by the great 18th century Kabbalist known as the Master of the Good Name—in Hebrew, the Baal Shem Tov:

A man or woman who is really pure cannot see any evil or wrongdoing in anyone else. Nor will a pure soul hear anything bad about anybody else. Any kind of negativity or evil will not be in that person's consciousness.

Therefore, states the Master of the Good Name, when people do see wrong or evil, they should know and understand, without a shadow of doubt, that they have something of that evil nature within themselves. In order for the person who has committed the wrongdoing to correct himself or herself, the person who witnessed this wrongdoing or repeated the gossip must first do his or her own correction.

A heavy responsibility! Not only do we affect our own lives, but our actions and words deeply touch the lives of others. There is a saying that no snowflake in an avalanche ever feels responsible.

THE MIRROR

Suppose there was a mirror that reflected all your negative character traits, all the reactive instincts you came to this world to transform. Now suppose you smashed the mirror and broke it into 1,000 little pieces. Each piece would reflect a different negative characteristic of your nature. Now suppose you scattered all those pieces all over the place. Guess what? All the negative people in your life, all the negative situations and obstacles that you confront, all the things you see wrong in others, are merely additional pieces of that mirror. Each fragment represents a different reflection of your own character. When you fix and transform a particular piece of your character, a fragment of mirror will reflect this transformation. You will begin to see the positive aspects of other people. Situations will begin to change for the better.

Remember that everything in your life is there for one reason and one reason only: to offer you the opportunity to transform. Transformation is the only way to effect positive change in your life and in this world. Stop wasting your energy finding fault in others. Start the transformation within. Start looking for the uncomfortable situations in life and avoiding the easy routes. The Light will be found only in the rough waters of life. Why? Because choppy seas trigger reactions.

Sure, it'll be turbulent for a while. You'll be buffeted from all sides at first. But if you remain certain that you are only being tested and if you don't react, the seas will calm down quickly. And that's when you'll come to know the power of Kabbalah. That's when you'll experience an extraordinary Light that has been trying to reach you and give you everything you've ever desired since time began.

And so we come to the Thirteenth Principle:

All of the negative traits that you spot in others are merely a reflection of your own negative traits. Only by fixing yourself can you change others.

IN CONCLUSION: GO AND LEARN

Trying to live our lives in a manner of complete accountability is perhaps the most difficult of all tasks. Our opponent will be there every step of the way. He makes gossip tempting and delicious. It will feel so much better to find wrong in others than to look in the mirror and find those same wrongs in ourselves. Our opponent blinds us to our own faults. We find it extremely difficult to detect them, let alone admit to them. So here is some advice from the mystics who mastered the secrets of our mysterious universe: No longer are we to consider ourselves victims. From this point onward we must accept responsibility for the rotten stuff that happens in our lives. We must admit that we are the cause. We must realize that we alone, by way of our previous actions, knowingly or unknowingly, have invited situations and people into our lives that will illuminate and bring out all of our destructive traits that we came here to transform.

This represents a profound and dramatic shift in human consciousness. It goes against every inclination and natural tendency in our instinctive nature. It means we are the cause of every chaotic moment in our lives. It means we recognize ourselves as the cause of our own misfortune. In case you've forgotten, being the cause is one of the main attributes of being proactive. And as we've learned throughout this book, becoming proactive is the ultimate purpose of our existence.

Thus, when we transcend past our inborn power of impulse; when we rise above the impelling force of animal instinct; when we stop pointing the finger of blame at someone else and, instead, clench a fist and strike a stunning blow to our real opponent in the game of life, we will make contact with the 99 percent realm. We will connect ourselves to an infinite, endless emanation of Light. We will have invoked the infinite power of God in our lives. And then the awesome power to change anything and everything will, at once, be placed in the palms of our hands.

WHEN ALL IS SAID AND DONE

There is a final and fourteenth principle for the game of life. This one secret embodies and embraces all the principles we have learned thus far.

If you have trouble remembering all the lessons laid out in this book, the Kabbalists gave us a unique bit of wisdom that contains all the other principles within it. It's like a magic secret and it is revealed to us by way of an old Kabbalistic parable that goes something like this:

A student approaches his revered teacher and master and asks him to teach him all the sublime secrets and magnificent mysteries of the cosmos in the short time that it takes to remain balanced on one leg. This eminent master is one of the greatest spiritual giants to ever walk this earth. Upon hearing his eager student's request, he considers the question very carefully. His eyes then sparkle with infinite wisdom...

"Love thy neighbor as thyself.

All the rest is mere commentary.

Now go and learn."

APPENDIX: KABBALAH'S 14 SPIRITUAL PRINCIPLES

1. Don't believe a word you read. Test-drive the lessons learned.

2. Two Basic Realities Exist: Our 1 Percent World of Darkness & the 99 Percent Realm of Light!

3. Everything that a human being truly desires from life is spiritual Light!

4. The purpose of life is spiritual transformation from a reactive being to a proactive being.

5. In the moment of our transformation we make contact with the 99 percent realm!

6. Never—and that means never—lay blame on other people or external events.

7. Resisting our reactive impulses creates lasting Light.

8. Reactive behavior creates intense sparks of Light, but eventually leaves darkness in its wake.

9. Obstacles are our opportunity to connect to

the Light

10. The greater the obstacle, the greater the potential Light.

11. When challenges appear overwhelming, inject certainty. The Light is always there!

12. True internal change is created through the DNA power of the Hebrew letters.

13. All of the negative traits that you spot in others are merely a reflection of your own negative traits. Only by fixing yourself can you change others.

And finally, ultimately:

14. Love thy neighbor as thyself. All the rest is mere commentary.

Now go and learn.

A BRIEF HISTORY OF KABBALAH

2000 B.C.E

The first written work on Kabbalah, called *The Book of Formation*, was authored by Abraham the Patriarch more than 4,000 years ago. *The Book of Formation* is said to contain all the mysteries of the universe, yet it is only a few pages long. How can that be?

Of course, a great deal can be shown in a concise way, as Einstein proved with his famous formula, $E=MC^2$. Within these five characters are mathematical insights that help define and explain the mysteries of time, space, energy, and matter. *The Book of Formation* is another such formula.

Just as it requires true mathematical knowledge to understand Einstein's formula, only those who were adept in the mystical arts of Kabbalah were able to penetrate the secrets within this holy book.

SECOND CENTURY CE

In the second century, there lived a remarkable mystic by the name of Rabbi Shimon bar Yochai. This giant among Kabbalists revealed a much more lengthy body of knowledge on Kabbalah called the *Zohar*. The *Zohar* was a profoundly spiritual work that explained all the secrets contained in *The Book of Formation*. The manuscript however, was considered mysticism and magic by the people of its generation.

In hindsight, the reason is obvious:

The *Zohar* expounds upon ideas and concepts that were centuries ahead of their time.

In an age where science determined the world was flat, The *Zohar* depicts our planet as spherical, with people experiencing day and night in different time zones.

The *Zohar* describes the moment of creation as a Big Bang–like explosion.

It speaks of a universe that exists in ten dimensions.

It explores the notion of parallel universes.

These speculations were heretical and frightening.

Yet, they are not the most fantastic to appear in the *Zohar*.

That designation belongs to another idea...

Rabbi Shimon says the *Zohar* is more than a book of secrets and spiritual wisdom.

This mystical treatise is a powerful energy-giving instrument; a life-saving tool that, in and of itself, is imbued with the power to bring genuine peace, protection, healing, and fulfillment to those who possess the actual physical books.

There's more.

Like the monolith in the film *2001: A Space Odyssey*, the *Zohar* can spark the soul of a generation, igniting profound change and transformation within the consciousness of human beings and society. In other words, just as a light bulb illumines a darkened room revealing objects previously unseen, the spiritual Light of the *Zohar* can enlighten the minds of humans to the hidden mysteries of the cosmos. According to the Kabbalists, these unseen influences will eventually help shape the destiny of humankind as the *Zohar*'s presence widens in our world.

The great sage Yochai stated that there would come a day when even a six-year-old child would be able to delve into the spiritual wisdom of Kabbalah. But until that time arrived, the original manuscripts of the *Zohar* had to remain concealed.

They were then hidden away for centuries. The dimming of the *Zohar*'s spiritual Light coincides with the Dark Ages, a time where every aspect of civilization including education, science and communications were in severe decline.

13TH CENTURY
KABBALIST R. MOSES DELEON

The great Spanish Kabbalist named Moses
Deleon made a startling discovery by uncovering the
Zohar manuscripts in a cave in Israel. The recent
discovery of the Dead Sea Scrolls pales in
comparison to the unearthing of the *Zohar* in terms
of spiritual significance. Rabbi Shimon wrote that
the concealment would last 1,200 years, beginning
from the time of the destruction of the Holy
Temple. The Temple in Jerusalem was destroyed by
Romans in the year 70 B.C.E. Moses Deleon
revealed the *Zohar* in the year 1270—1,200 years
later, as Rabbi Shimon had anticipated.

Moses Deleon's discovery generally went
unnoticed by the world. But it's a historically
significant turning point as the Light of the *Zohar*
radiates into the world for the first time in human
history. Its arcane verses render the work inaccessible
to the masses. However, Kabbalists believe that the
energy emanating from its mystical text sparked the
collective unconscious of a generation. Some five
years after Deleon published the *Zohar* c.1275,
famed philosopher Roger Bacon foresaw a future

where ships would travel underwater, machines would fly in the sky, and boats would voyage without sails or oars. It sounded a lot like mysticism to the people who dwelt in his generation, and Roger Bacon was soon imprisoned for heresy.

Not long after, Nicholas Oresme, philosopher, economist, mathematician, physicist, and one of the principal founders of modern science, taught about the motion of the earth, 200 years before Copernicus. He wrote about the nature of light, reflection of light, and the speed of light—concepts explored at great length by the *Zohar*. Nicholas invented coordinate geometry long before Descartes, and he discovered that all objects plunge to the ground at the same speed long before Galileo "discovered" the same thing. For some reason, Copernicus, Descartes, and Galileo all received top billing in the history books while good old Nicholas is practically a footnote.

16TH CENTURY

The 16th century Kabbalist, Isaac Luria, was a child prodigy who delved deeply into the mystical wonders of the *Zohar*. Nicknamed "the Ari," or the Holy Lion, he produced a commentary on the *Zohar* that removed another layer of its complexity. The Ari's teachings become the definitive school of Kabbalistic thought. All the material in this book is rooted in Lurianic Kabbalah. Also in the 16th century, in 1540, the Kabbalist Abraham Azulai issued a decree that removed any and all Resistances concerning the learning of Kabbalah. This would be the first time in human history that Kabbalah could be made available to everyone, even a six-year-old child.

17TH CENTURY—A KABBALISTIC SCIENTIFIC REVOLUTION

The 17th century experienced an abrupt and unexplainable explosion of scientific advancement, yet scholars and scientists alike have been hard pressed to find the reason for this impromptu happening. On the basis of new evidence, however, scholars now argue that Kabbalah had a profound influence on many of the great scientists and mathematicians of the 17th century—a time when the lines between philosophy and science, physics and metaphysics, were completely blurred. Professor Allison P. Coudert contends in her book, *The Impact of the Kabbalah* in the Seventeenth Century, that "Lurianic Kabbalah deserves a place it has never received in the histories of western scientific and cultural developments."

The great mathematician Leibniz, who concurrently with Sir Isaac Newton invented calculus and, in turn, those tiresome math classes we endured in high school, was profoundly influenced by Kabbalah. So was Newton, the man most responsible for the scientific revolution and the launching of the Age of Enlightenment. And it's probable that Galileo, Descartes, Plato, and Copernicus were also exposed to the knowledge of Kabbalah.

Leibniz, considered one of the great intellects of the period, believed that Kabbalah personified a primordial secret wisdom (*prisca theologia*) that God had secretly revealed to Moses on Mount Sinai (sound familiar?). Leibniz, Newton, and their peers believed that if the pure Kabbalah was rediscovered and revealed to the world in its genuine, uncorrupted form, it would bring about universal peace by establishing a foundation for a true ecumenical religion, thereby eradicating the religious conflicts that have left the landscape of human civilization soiled in blood.

EARLY 20ᵀᴴ CENTURY

But it was not until the start of the 20th century that Kabbalist Rav Yehuda Ashlag, the most profound mystic of this century, deciphered the writings of the Ari and the texts of the *Zohar*. Now the wisdom of Kabbalah was more accessible than ever before, which, by the way, did not please certain factions in the religious community. In one of many cruel incidents, Rav Ashlag was left lying in a pool of his own blood on the steps of his Learning Centre. Undaunted, Rav Ashlag delved into Lurianic Kabbalah with devout fervor and unraveled its greatest secrets. But the vast majority of the world paid little attention to his historic action, nor could they perceive its influence. Concepts such as relativity, space travel, healing, parallel universes, and matters affecting the welfare of humankind were encoded into the *Zohar* some 2,000 years ago. The *Zohar's* emergence into the secular world occurred in a century that saw more technological advancements than all other centuries combined. Rav Ashlag's genius lay in his ability to extrapolate these secrets from the Ari's 500-year-old writings.

The sage's greatest legacy is the first Hebrew

translation of the *Zohar* from its original Aramaic, along with his famous commentary. Befitting a man of his spiritual stature, Rav Ashlag left this world on Yom Kippur night, in 1955.

MID 20TH CENTURY

Rav Ashlag's chief disciple, Kabbalist Yehudah Brandwein, completed and published his master's monumental writings. Though pious and orthodox, Rav Brandwein was a man of the common people, especially the disenfranchised. He was a gentle and humble soul who scaled scaffolding on construction sites by day and then scaled lofty spiritual worlds by moonlight. Rav Brandwein embraced everyone he met, regardless of their religious observances or absence of them, with unconditional love and acceptance. He evoked a deep love in all those with whom he came in contact. Both atheists and devout believers had great reverence for him. Rav Brandwein left this world in 1969, after having passed the sacred torch to his beloved student, Kabbalist Rav Berg.

THE PRESENT DAY

Continuing the teachings of Rav Ashlag and those of his own master, Rav Brandwein, Rav Berg and his wife, Karen Berg, broke with 2,000 years of tradition and religious dogma and brought the wisdom of Kabbalah within the reach of everyone who had a sincere desire to learn. This daring act was not without cost. Like most of the Kabbalists throughout history, Rav Berg and Karen endured physical violence, extreme verbal abuse, and emotional pain and suffering at the hands of those who were determined to keep the secrets of Kabbalah from the likes of you and me—regular people who sought answers from religion that went beyond the traditional response—"*Because it is written.*" Because Rav Berg and Karen opened the ancient vaults of Kabbalah to the masses, people everywhere now have an opportunity to understand why we exist, how we arrived here, and how we can remove pain, suffering, torment, fear, and chaos from our personal lives. The secret is finally out and that is why you were able to read this book.